7000 MILES

TO FREEDOM

NAZ MEKNAT

Black Rose Writing | Texas

ISBN: 978-1-68433-807-8
PUBLISHED BY BLACK ROSE WRITING
www.blackrosewriting.com

Printed in the United States of America
Suggested Retail Price (SRP) $17.95

7000 Miles to Freedom is printed in EB Garamond

*As a planet-friendly publisher, Black Rose Writing does its best to eliminate unnecessary waste to reduce paper usage and energy costs, while never compromising the reading experience. As a result, the final word count vs. page count may not meet common expectations.

"For those who fought for it, freedom has a taste the protected will never know"

For my Family, without you, I would be lost.

7000 MILES
TO FREEDOM

In this book, I tell my personal story and write about events, places and situations as I experienced them. Other people might have perceived similar circumstances differently. This book relates my individual journey and only reflects my own perspective. **–Naz Meknat**

INTRODUCTION

A Girl with a Dream

"What you seek is seeking you."
–Rumi

Awakened from a deep sleep, I rolled over in my Cannes hotel suite bed, taking in the view of the Mediterranean Sea. Its sparkling turquoise waters were dappled with sunlight, blending into deep lapis blue towards the horizon as if the scene had been freshly painted by some Monet or Impressionist Master.

It was May 15, 2016, just a few days after my 42nd birthday. I had intended to sleep in, but at 7:30 am I was disturbed by the sound of my friend Mia frantically trying to put herself together as best she could before heading to her job at the American Pavilion during the Cannes Film Festival.

I was completely awake now, so I propped myself up on the pillows and looked out through the sliding glass window next to my bed, watching the early risers strolling along the Promenade de la Croisette and admiring the billionaires' yachts anchored in the distance. It suddenly occurred to me that this would be my last day here, and I felt a tinge of sadness. I wished to stay until the end of the film festival, but I had to return to Los Angeles and tend to the rest of my clients back home.

Without giving it, another thought I jumped out of bed and decided to make the most out of my last day in Cannes. I had visited this beautiful coastal town on the French Riviera on a previous occasion, during a trip across Europe with an ex-boyfriend, but something magical happened here during the film festival. The mixture of stunning views, the beauty of Cannes, the amazing food and my love of cinema and fashion made this place feel like a corner of paradise at this particular time.

In the week we had spent here, I had established a delicious routine. Every morning after our standard Parisian breakfast of coffee, croissants, and fruit on the balcony, enjoying the azure view, Mia would rush off to work while I finished getting ready. Then I would leisurely make my way over to my celebrity clients' nearby hotel to get them ready for their day of press junkets, interviews, photo-shoots and red-carpet events.

If I finished early enough, I would stroll over to join Mia at the American Pavilion, where I would set up my laptop and attempt to do admin for my styling business courtesy of the free Wi-Fi at the Pavilion. I had to answer e-mails, check with my assistant, make appointments and sometimes attend virtual fittings with clients back in Los Angeles.

At times it was hard to focus with the energy around me at the pavilion. Directors, producers, people from financing panels, and the Screen Actors Guild were constantly milling about, making deals, and conducting round table discussions. Lighting, hair, and makeup people were flitting back and forth, setting up a photoshoot for People and other magazines. The tent was a hive of nonstop activity. I enjoyed the opportunity to sit there quietly and observe the restless commotion. At times, I would take a stroll by the row of tents that represented the different countries participating in the festival that year and poke my head in the tents to see how other countries were conducting their business. I even made some great friends.

On this last day, with no more celebrity styling duties, I decided to take a leisurely walk around this sparkling seaside gem and explore the town, taking in all the color and beauty. I walked through the narrow alleys and stopped by every small shop, carefully examining the goods, trying to find some meaningful souvenirs to take back home for my family and friends. I stopped at a café and I could not stop myself from sampling a delicious pastry with my espresso. I talked myself out of the guilt by convincing my conscience that it was the last day and I could therefore eat all the pastries I wanted. Soon I would be back in Los Angeles, my city, where the hunt for a mildly decent croissant always proved unsuccessful.

Walking by the designer boutiques and looking through the windows, I was tempted to go inside and try on a few items from the newest collections only available on the European market. But I could not indulge in such a careless splurge and stopped instead by another dreamlike bakery, opting to eat the luxury rather than wear it.

When I returned to my hotel room later that day I headed straight to the balcony, sat on a chair, and got lost in my thoughts, wondering what my last night in Cannes would entail. Maybe dinner at a new spot with a few friends or drinks at the lobby bar of Hotel Martinez or Hotel Le Majestic?

I was deep in this pleasant reverie when Mia burst into the room and called out to me, "Naz!" she exclaimed. At first, I thought there had been some sort of crisis. I noticed she was breathing hard as if she had just run a marathon.

"What is it? What's wrong?" I asked her.

"You know that amazing black gown you brought but didn't get to wear?" she said.

"Yes," I replied, puzzled.

She was referring to a black mermaid-style gown with matte black scales that I had borrowed from a designer showroom in Los Angeles where I usually got red carpet gowns or tuxedos for my clients. The showroom owner, a young French woman who had known me for years, had let me pick a couple of gowns to take with me for the festival. I had been dying to wear this dress, but the occasion for such a fancy gown had not arisen.

"Tonight is the night you are wearing it," she announced with the biggest smile.

"No way! What are we doing?" I asked, still not believing she was serious.

"You and I will be going to the Premier of 'Hands of Stone'!" Mia said as she threw her hands in the air with excitement.

I stared at her shocked, "What?! Are you serious?"

"Happy Birthday Naz!" she said with a big smile. "And that's not all," she continued, "We are going to the after-party too".

Robert De Niro's movie was one of the most anticipated films in the whole festival. I ran and gave her a big hug, "Oh my god, Mia! How did you make that happen? This is fantastic."

She just smiled and said, "Get ready my friend, we don't have much time."

I was giddy with excitement in anticipation of this star-studded event. Walking the red carpet at Cannes Film Festival, climbing the iconic stairs at the Palais des Festivals et des Congress, attending the premiere and the after-party with the cast... I was about to live out my dreams.

It was already after 6:00 PM and we were due to arrive by 7:30 PM. Factoring in the travel time through the limo traffic and rush of people, I figured I had less than an hour to get myself dolled up. I showered quickly, fixed my hair and makeup in record time, then slipped into the most beautiful dress I had ever worn. It fitted my body perfectly, as if it was made especially for me. I paused for a second to check myself in the full-length mirror by the door and I took it all in.

I was always the one behind the scenes: It was my job to get actors and actresses looking flawless for the red carpet. But now I was going to be the one walking alongside the stars with hundreds of photographers taking pictures.

On our ride to the Palais, I felt butterflies in my stomach. I had never experienced such excitement. I used these few moments of silence in the backseat of our black SUV to compose myself. God forbid I should look anything but cool. "Be calm!", I urged myself.

"Okay, Mesdames, we have arrived. Please watch your step," the driver announced before swinging around to open the car door for us.

A true gentleman, he held our hands to help us out of the car and make sure we did not fall. Red-carpet moments can be rather disorienting and we needed his steady hand, especially in the sky-high pair of heels we both were wearing. All I could see was the flashbulbs of the cameras going off. I could hear the screaming fans as reporters interviewed the stars.

I felt slightly shy as we made our way through the melee towards the famous stairs. My first impulse was to run up the stairs, away from the madness, preferably without tripping. But photographers kept shouting at me to stop so they could take a picture. That dress was getting me far more attention than I was used to getting. One photographer went as far as claiming I was the best-dressed woman on the carpet. I was not so sure about that. Many beautiful A-list actresses from all around the world were walking the carpet in stunning couture gowns, but I thanked him for the compliment anyway.

When we reached the top of the stairs I stopped, turned, and looked at the view behind me. It was a scene of a beautiful chaos. I seized that Cinderella moment to reflect for an instant.

How did I get here? Was this real? Was I dreaming? It was an unbelievable scene. I was shoulder to shoulder with some of the biggest stars in the world, attending one of the most prestigious events of the year. My heart was overwhelmed with gratitude and I was speechless.

I looked down to hide my teary eyes and caught a glimpse of the old scars on my bare arms. A wave of emotion came over me. I was reminded of the pain, of the struggle, of the life I had to escape. I had a flashback to the dark days, the lonely nights, the monsters who tried repeatedly to crush my soul, and the nightmare I left behind in order to find myself. With everything I had gone through, I could have ended up dead or in a dark place—a deep hole that I could not climb out of. Instead, I was living this fairytale life. I was experiencing what I dreamed of as a child, looking at the pictures of glamorous Hollywood stars walking up these stairs, mesmerized by the beautiful gowns and shiny diamonds. It seemed out of reach for a girl like me, yet here I was.

More than anything, I felt proud. Proud of never giving up, never allowing myself to feel like a victim, never letting people keep me down, and always finding a way to get back up.

This ordinary girl who had to fight for the right to a simple life was now walking amongst the rich, the famous and the privileged. Except nothing about my life had been ordinary. I had suffered plenty, but now it was all behind me. All that was left of my past life were fading scars.

I had to let go of the bitterness in order to be free and abandon the deep-seated resentment towards those who wronged me. To build this life for myself, I had to release these negative feelings. No one was going to do it for me, I had to face my own demons and find peace with the past.

Deep in my thoughts, I felt a hand reaching for mine. I looked up, gave Mia's hand a squeeze as a sign that I was fine. We turned around and walked inside to take our seats.

This is where I leave the pain behind; today is when I change the narrative. My scars are not a reminder of suffering anymore. They signal my strength and my resilience. They will always be with me, demonstrating that I did not just survive but I thrived.

This is my story, the story of how I made it from there... to here.

CHAPTER ONE

Portrait of a City

"Time is a factory where everyone slaves away
earning enough love to break their own chains."
–Hafiz

As she tugged me along the rubble-strewn streets of Tehran, I grasped my mother's hand for dear life. I had no idea where we were headed, and she was moving so fast that I was frightened of getting left behind in the crowd. People passing by in a rush on the crowded sidewalk could barely see my small figure trying to keep up with my mother's brisk pace. A few long blocks later, she stopped abruptly outside a barbershop.

She turned to me and bent down low so I could hear her better.

"You are going to get your head shaved today", she said

I looked up at her, bewildered.

"Don't worry. It won't hurt and your hair will grow back sooner than you think. And when it does, it will be full, shiny and strong,"

There was nothing to do but obey. My five-year-old self knew better than to question Mom when she had a notion about what was best for me. She believed, like many Iranian mothers, that in some magical way my fine hair would grow back thick and luscious if shaved only once. All my cousins, from both my mom and dad's side, had long, lustrous manes of dark hair. But neither I nor my sisters had inherited this trait.

In our culture, a girl was only as good as her beauty and her domestic skills. This remained true even after the Iranian Revolution, when Islamic law dictated that we cover our assets with a hijab. Not many cared about a girl's level of education or intelligence back then. The most important thing, once you reached a certain age, was to be marriage material, and my mother was determined I would be ready when the time came.

I sat in the barber's chair meekly while he buzzed my scalp bare and watched in disbelief as my wispy brown tresses gently fell to the floor. Shocked, I stared at my new image in the mirror. I was now a bald 5-year-old girl. My skinny frame looked even smaller with no hair.

On the walk home I bowed my head in embarrassment, convinced that everyone was staring at this freakish little bare-headed girl and passing judgement. I avoided eye contact the entire time, hoping this would somehow make me invisible.

When we got home, I ran to the room I was sharing with my much older sisters, sat in front of the mirror and stared again at my reflection, trying to recognize the little girl with no hair staring back at me. I ran my hand over my naked head back and forth, trying unsuccessfully to get used to the feeling. I felt naked without my long locks.

For a few days, I refused to go out for any reason and stayed inside, deeply ashamed of my new look. But eventually, I got bored. Watching the neighborhood boys playing soccer on the street from our living room window gave me an idea. With no hair to define my gender, I could easily pass as a boy. I could pretend to be one of them and join in on their fun. This lifted my spirits and gave me renewed confidence. I was convinced I could fool them.

In Iran, little girls were expected to play inside, learning how to sew, cook and knit from their mothers and grandmothers, but I chafed against those restraints. I was never interested in playing with Barbies. The plastic mini tea set and dolls I was given stayed in the closet and collected dust over time. Long before I fully understood social expectations and felt the pressure to conform to gender roles, I avoided pretend-cooking-and-cleaning games.

For the most part, I was a tomboy—at least by Iranian standards. I liked to be outdoors, climb trees and ride my bike. Above all, I loved to play soccer. Shortly after I was born, my family had moved to the downstairs section of a two-story house in a quiet residential street close to bustling downtown Tehran. Away from the traffic, boys could play freely out in the street until the sun went down. Watching from my window, I had always envied them. My buzz cut gave me an opportunity to be accepted as one of them.

I put on a pair of pants and a T-shirt, went to my mom who was busy in the kitchen preparing food, as she did three times a day, and asked her,

"Can I go play outside?"

The answer was no at first, but she relented after seeing the sad, defeated look on my face. She had a lot to do around the house and no time to argue with a willful 5-year-old.

"You can go, but stay where I can see you," she told me.

Cheered by my victory, I rushed outside and jauntily walked up to the kid who appeared in charge of the soccer group. I introduced myself as a new boy in the neighborhood.

"Hi, I am Saeed, I'm Naz's cousin, can I play too?"

The kids paused their game. The lead boy—a short, chubby kid named Omid who was a couple of years older than me—looked me up and down. His clothes were stained, and he had dirt all over his face and body.

Glancing at the other boys, he started laughing. The rest of the team followed suit. Of course, they weren't fooled. But even if they didn't believe me, I was not about to give up that easily. I stood there firmly, trying to convey that I meant business, and asked again. Omid eventually agreed to let me play on one condition: if I turned out to be a really bad player, the team would kick me out. No appeal! I promised to play my best game. I was allowed to play goalie, and I was damn good at it.

During those next few weeks, I experienced pure, unadulterated joy. I started walking and talking like a boy with my new soccer friends, begged my dad to teach me how to whistle, and insisted on being called Saeed—a popular name for boys.

I was having the time of my life. The youngest child in the family, separated from my siblings by big age gaps, I could not relate to them in any way or share their activities. As a result, I was often alone. Playing with my new friends, I enjoyed the companionship and discovered my competitive side. I loved the rough and tumble, which made me feel freer and more confident that at any other time in my short life. Kicking a ball with the neighborhood boys, I had found my happy place.

In a way, that early experience marked me and toughened me up. It was the first time I had to bluff my way through a difficult situation to be accepted and respected. This first test of my life was an important lesson that I would later use to survive. Little did I know at the time how many more tests I could have to pass during my youth.

•   •   •

My country was still recovering from the aftermath of a bloody revolution, one of the most tumultuous events in its history.

At a young age, I witnessed disturbing scenes. A year earlier, I had seen dead bodies on street corners and bloody hand marks on the walls as helicopters hovered overhead. I remember Mom urging me to run faster on my spindly legs as we rushed home to safety after being caught up unaware in a demonstration when returning from shopping for food. She tried to shield me from the gory sights but offered no explanation for the turmoil I was witnessing.

Protesters occupied the streets day after day, chanting slogans—some of them anti-government and some pro-Shah. Tension was high and the sound of gunshots resonated as the two groups clashed and troops intervened.

As a young child, I did not understand what was going on but the air felt heavy with fear and uncertainty. The adults around me looked permanently preoccupied and spoke in hushed tones. The TV in our living-room stayed on round the clock so my parents could keep up with what was happening in Tehran and all over our country. Outside, momentous events were unfolding that would have a direct impact on all citizens, but particularly women and girls. They not only shaped my childhood, but my entire life and that of millions of others.

At the height of the revolution, my dad forbade all family members from stepping outside. It was simply too dangerous.

After over a year of demonstrations, riots and strikes that brought life at a standstill across the country, the Shah, already weakened by the cancer that would kill him the next year, was finally overthrown and left Iran in February 1979. Some officers switched sides and joined the revolutionaries; others fled the country fearing for their lives as Islamic fundamentalists clerics, known as the Mullahs, took over, led by Ayatollah Khomeini.

The revolution marked a radical break with the country's glorious past, even if the Pahlavi dynasty had only come to power in the 1920s when the Shah's father, a military officer was crowned following a coup. In the eyes of many Iranians proud of an ancient culture that stretched back several millennia, the great Persian Empire, a cradle of art and science for centuries, had collapsed in front of their eyes.

.   .   .

I never really knew life before the revolution. I was just a small child starting to come into my own at the time. But for my parents and their generation, life would be forever divided between a "before" and "after" period. Young kids like me accepted the restrictions imposed by the Islamic regime as the "normal" we grew up with, but as I reached adolescence, these limitations began to weigh heavily.

My dad, who was very traditional but not religious, fiercely opposed the Mullahs. He foresaw that the situation would deteriorate after their takeover and warned my older siblings to stay away from the protests.

To the outside world, post-revolutionary Iran appeared blanketed in a thick cover of religion. But many households had not wanted this change. Inside the country, many families, ours included, were trying to salvage what they could of their prior lives.

As I got older, I gradually noticed how different our living conditions were from the rest of the world. I kept asking questions, confounded and curious to find out why some of my compatriots had brought this repressive regime upon themselves and the rest of us.

I could not understand why Iranian people had willingly gave up their freedoms and rights in exchange for a religious extremist rule that stripped them of their most basic human rights. I needed answers, but no one had good explanations to offer. Everyone just offered wild conspiracy theories or blamed someone else. The country was deeply divided, and daily living circumstances were getting worse.

Much later—long after I had left Iran—I understood that the situation in Iran before the revolution had been more complex than I thought. The Shah was authoritarian and many of the revolution's early supporters had hoped that the regime change would bring greater democratic rights, only to see their aspirations brutally crushed by the Mullahs.

As a young girl from a middle-class family, I grew up under tight control from the authorities. From how to speak to how we should dress and behave, every step was dictated. The regime killed individuality and every citizen was expected to conform with the religious rules that the government enforced. Women and girls had to always wear loose clothes in drab colors. Civilians were watched closely, and disobedience was harshly punished. God forbid we showed the shape of our body! Our hair had to be fully covered.

For someone like me who enjoyed theater, dancing, painting, music and grew up dreaming of movies and colorful fashion, the environment was stifling.

Throughout my youth, the streets were under the control of the religious Islamic police—a zealous vice squad formed to keep people in check and ensure compliance with religious observance and public morality rules on behalf of the authorities. Committee members, often recruited from poor and uneducated families and brainwashed with the promise of power and money, roamed all over the city in unmarked SUVs. Armed with guns and batons, they had the authority to beat people, young and old, male or female, and arrest them for behavior they consider immoral. Female squads of women dressed from head to toe in black *chadors* that covered them like tents were among the most ardent enforcers. Even laughing in public was seen as unruly behavior, particularly for women. For most of us with more modern views, growing up in that environment felt like a life sentence in a maximum-security prison.

• • •

Since enjoying life in public was against the law, when I was a teenager we held our own underground parties and got together in the privacy of our homes. We drank liquor that someone's uncle had secretly made in their basement or perhaps someone's dad had smuggled from Europe. Some of the home-made brews tasted foul and were concocted with unsuitable ingredients, such a medicinal alcohol, that made them dangerous. But drinking provided an escape.

We listened to music, illegally because Western music was prohibited. Girls and boys mixed together, danced, smoked cigarettes, and sang along to the latest pop music. At parties, girls would arrive wearing the required "manteau", a shapeless coat in a dark color, their heads fully covered in the roosari (headscarf) demanded by the authorities. As soon as they stepped inside, they shed their outer layers to reveal Western clothes and long hair. Some of us brought party clothes and makeup in plastic bags.

The rest of the time, Iranian youth gathered in coffee shops—with genders seated at separate tables, of course, but close enough to exchange a few words—or drove around Tehran aimlessly, particularly in the northern, fancier part of the city.

In short, we made the most of a horrible situation under the beady eyes of the clerics that ruled us. These distractions from the difficulties of daily life were not without risk. While we were having fun, we prayed that the Morality Police would not burst into our homes and arrest us all. Unfortunately, this happened often. The consequences were dire—anyone caught attending a mixed-gender gathering where liquor was served could get severely punished, usually through flogging. Some of those detained were whipped until their flesh looked as raw as a piece of uncooked meat. The authorities justified this inhumane treatment of people in the name of religion. Having fun was a crime!

Despite my rebellious nature, I was among the lucky people who never to experience flogging myself. I am honestly not sure if my petite and thin frame would have survived it. I did have my fair share of troubles with the authorities but I was never sentenced to prison or forced to suffer that barbaric form of physical punishment. However, I am certain that if I had stayed in my country any longer than I did, I would have come into conflict with these authorities and would probably have been imprisoned and silenced because of my unrelenting will to speak the truth.

My brother Joseph, on the other hand, was not as fortunate as I was. He got arrested many times, either for attending parties or for the way he dressed in public. One day, he got stopped in the street and taken into custody for wearing a T-shirt with a printed picture of an American heavy metal band, sent from the US by our older sister Niloo. In most countries, people wear what they want without a second thought, but not in Iran.

The injustice did not stop there. One night, the Morality Police, guns drawn, stormed a private party where guests had been listening to music and dancing the night away. My brother Joseph ran upstairs, snuck out through a window and took off jumping from rooftop to rooftop. He knew that his record would count against him and he would not get off easily if he was arrested. He had been in trouble with the religious police too many times and they were watching him. He got caught a few blocks down the road and was brought to the police station.

This time, he was lashed repeatedly and savagely. He stumbled into our parents' apartment, in shock and excruciating pain, barely able to speak. Raw flesh was visible under the wide cuts to the skin. Joseph's back remained bloody and painful for days. Mom's screams, when she saw what the authorities had done to her only son, still resonate in my ears. She collapsed in floods of tears. We all knew that protesting was not possible. Anyone who complained or spoke up against these anachronistic rules risked the same treatment. We lived in fear and had no choice but to keep silent in the face of such injustice.

. . .

A year after the revolution, Iraq's dictator Saddam Hussein took advantage of Iran's vulnerable situation and attacked our soil. With evil intent to promote Arab nationalism and economic expansion, he launched a conflict against Iran that lasted eight years, caused massive bloodshed and unleashing a wave of collective grief.

The war hit us hard: After the revolution, the Iranian population was tired. As the conflict went on, the economy worsened, reducing a country that was once one of the richest in the region to substandard living conditions. Sadness, uncertainty and unspoken fear lingered over the whole country.

As young children, we were not spared the war's impact. One of my cousins died at the front, his death a traumatic loss for my extended family. Following bombing raids on Tehran, school friends living nearby stopped attending class. We learned later that they had died when their home took a direct hit.

During my childhood and teenage years, when I was not losing friends or family members to the bombs and rockets dropped onto civilians by the Iraqi air force, they disappeared because they were moving to other parts of the world. Anyone who found an opportunity to escape the dire situation took all they could and fled the country—at least, if they were privileged enough to seize their chance.

The majority of the Jewish community fled Iran in fear for their lives under an extremist Islamic regime, which declared Israel an enemy almost immediately after they seized power. Christians could no longer practice their religion freely and members of the small Baha'i community, who practiced their faith peacefully and quietly, found themselves persecuted and facing execution. Immigrating became the only hope of finding safety, freedom and a better life, particularly for families who feared their teenage sons drafted into the army.

. . .

In the meantime, those of us who stayed, tried to make life as tolerable as we could. In spite of the repression, people found ways to bypass the bans and strict rules.

Movie watching became a popular form of passive resistance to the mullahs' diktat. It was strictly prohibited and severely punished, but that did not stop us. There was even a hierarchy of sin: Hollywood movies, produced in the Great Satan country—the United States—drew particular scorn from the authorities. Possession of pre-revolutionary Iranian movies, however, incurred even harsher disciplinary measures. The regime wanted to erase the past.

From an early age, I was fascinated by films and would watch anything I could get my hands on. The only way we could access Western movies was by renting bootleg VHS tapes on the black market.

An ingenious system emerged: First, you had to be referred by someone trustworthy to a video trader—a brave soul who would show up at your house once a week with a briefcase containing the latest films, taking a huge risk. For a fee, you could choose up to three tapes from the limited selection of VHS cassettes available, mostly blockbusters. The man would faithfully come back the following week to exchange the tapes for different ones.

Every neighborhood had an assigned day of the week and the video man's visits were eagerly awaited in a city where entertainment was in short supply. The trade in pirated videos was no doubt lucrative, but it could result in years of imprisonment for the black marketeer if caught. We never knew the name of our video man and we had no way of contacting him directly.

Thanks to this shadowy network, we watched the Oscar and the Golden Globe award ceremonies on VHS tapes that were smuggled into the country in mysterious ways, months after the events. The recordings were often of poor quality, but the scratchy reels lit up our world like a ray of sunshine in darkness. No wonder the authorities worked hard to prevent us from watching them!

· · ·

News of our young men dying every day on the front lines of a war, mixed with the stress of life under the constant threat of extreme punishment, fostered a suspicious and hostile environment.

Fear was a part of everyday life and everyone always looked over their shoulder. I lost track of where most of my friends had ended up after fleeing the country. Some travelled to Germany, others to France, Australia, and some to Canada. They were scattered all around the world.

Families, including mine, were torn apart. One by one, my cousins and my siblings emigrated, out of necessity or simply the desire to live better.

Moving across the world as a refugee to start a new life in a foreign country was no easy feat. In most cases, you had to learn a new language, acquire new skills to find work and earn a living. Parents tried to save their children and help them get a better life, but it was hard to see them go. And when older people relocated, they struggled to start over in old age. They had to swallow their pride and lower their standards just to put food on the table and secure a safe home far away from their motherland. My parents, too, would eventually leave the country of their birth to move closer to their children in California. It was heartbreaking for them, though they were fortunate to do so when their adult children were already well established and able to ease their entry into US society.

Those of us living in Iran during the war years experienced hardship as the economy got hit so hard that the government introduced a rationing program nationwide. Every household, rich or poor, was allocated coupons, based on the size of their family. These were distributed by a government agency to ensure that the country did not run out of necessities and people didn't die from hunger.

Lines formed in front of designated stores that the government had acquired to distribute these supplies. People waited in the queue sometimes for hours, coupons in hand, to receive their weekly share of meat, bread, sugar, and other essential items.

Dad used to send me to stand in line to pick up his cigarettes. I was only about 10 at the time, but the people in charge of the distribution did not mind handing the cigarettes over to a child, as long as I mentioned that it was for my father. When the war came to a bitter end in 1988, the economy finally started to recover and basic items returned to the stores, but it was a slow process. The scars from the conflict with Iraq—like those of the Vietnam War in the US—lingered on in the society long after the conflict was over.

.   .   .

To mitigate the impact of the repression, many of us took up outdoor recreational activities. In broad open spaces, the likelihood of coming across the morality squad was lower. Courting couples adopted mountain hiking as a hobby that allowed them to spend time together in the great outdoors. Others simply wanted to escape the polluted atmosphere of the city and enjoy fresh air and exercise.

Roya, my second older sister was an enthusiastic hiker. I preferred skiing, which I discovered in my teens. This expensive sport was normally reserved for the rich, but I had wealthy friends who, during the winter season, frequently traveled to Dizin or Shemshak, the best ski resorts in the region, located only a couple of hours by car outside Tehran. For those who had the means, this was one of the most fun outdoors activities available.

My parents were not rich. Like most of our acquaintances, we were an ordinary middle-class family. But thanks to my more affluent friends, I was occasionally able to enjoy the high life normally reserved to a small percentage of privileged people. I loved it and wished I could always live that way!

Whenever I was invited, I begged my parents to allow me to join my friends and I saved every penny I was given for a chance to tag along on those ski trips. I wore ski clothes borrowed from my friends, stayed at their family cabin and used older ski equipment they had discarded. Since I could not afford to hire a ski instructor, I watched other skiers carefully and tried to mimic their moves. I was young, determined to blend in and fearless. At first, I fell often but I was a quick learner and got the hang of it.

Soon enough, skiing became one of my favorite hobbies. Going down the slope at speed with the cold crisp mountain air on my face gave me a sense of freedom that I could not experience elsewhere. I tried to act cool, as if I was one of the elite kids I hung out with. I desperately wanted to belong.

But the long arm of the Islamic regime even extended as far as the pristine ski slopes, which were sectioned into two separate parts—one side for women who had to keep their headscarf on under layers of ski clothing and the other for men. Even if they were married or with siblings, men and women had to ski separately.

When a group of us, boys and girls, traveled together, this caused logistical problems. If we wanted to meet up for lunch or a cup of tea with the guys, we had to agree on a time to meet at one of the restaurants or cafes. This was an era before everybody had their own smartphone— I am guessing the early brick-size cellphones already existed in America or other first-world countries at the time, but they had not yet reached our part of the world.

In public, we could not sit at the same table. But at the end of a day of fun in the snow, we would meet at the bottom of the slopes and head back to the cabin and hide behind closed doors. We had to make sure that the religious police could not find our mixed group of girls and boys. By staying together under the same roof, drinking vodka, playing cards and listening to western music, we infringed a long list of rules. But these trips provided memorable moments when we almost felt like normal teenagers.

· · ·

Close to Tehran, we were blessed with amazing natural resources that helped to keep us sane. Many of my American friends are surprised when I tell them I skied: They expect Tehran to be in the middle of a desert because it is in the Middle East. This is far from the truth.

Winters in Tehran were extremely cold, and we often had snow up to our knees and freezing temperatures. As school kids, after heavy snowfall overnight, we would sit by the radio in the morning to catch the newscast, hoping that schools would be closed that day due to snow blocking the roads. All of us in the neighborhood knew exactly what to do when we heard the cheerful news: We put on our snow boots and heavy jackets, met outside and played in the thick powdery snow all day.

Iran, as a matter of fact, enjoys a great diversity of landscapes and climates. In the north is the Caspian Sea, bordered by lush forests with breathtaking views of rivers and waterfalls. The southern part of the country is where you find sandy deserts and dry land.

My city, Tehran, sits in the foothills of the Alborz mountains where you could find small teahouses, outdoor garden restaurants and cafes right by the natural streams. I remember family outings and weekend getaways when I was little. Us kids would play by the water stream while adults sipped freshly brewed tea and smoked hookah. But as the war progressed, the mood darkened all over the country and festive outings became rarer.

When Nowrouz, the Persian new year arrives on March 20, the first day of spring, flowers bloom, trees are green, and the temperature is as good as it gets. In the summer, we escape the blistering heat of the city and travel north where the air is cooler, and the breeze of the Caspian Sea comforts your senses. In the fall, the whole city turns gold when the leaves turn yellow, and the sidewalks are covered in dry golden leaves.

One of my favorite childhood memories is walking back from school on those cool fall days playing a game that involved stepping on every dry and yellow leaf on the ground. The crunch of the leaves underfoot remains a familiar and soothing sound that feeds my soul. To this day, I cannot quit the habit of jumping on dry leaves. Onlookers may find it childish to see a grown woman skipping along on the pavement, but I could not care less because it reminds me of home and of the reassuring little things of everyday life that brought me joy in the middle of the fear and chaos.

I cannot forget the harsh reality and brutality we suffered under the tyrannical regime, but I cling to these few happy memories I have of my beautiful country and innocent childhood moments exploring nature's playground. I want to remember the kind and comforting beauty of my country. The pain inflected by my country must not displace these precious memories in my head.

I still hope that one day all of us, whether Muslim, Jewish, Christian, Baha'i or not practicing any religion like myself, can go back to our homeland without fear of getting killed, imprisoned or tortured simply because we want to enjoy basic human rights in the land of our birth.

CHAPTER TWO

Natural Born Rebel

"Stay close to anything that makes you glad you are alive."
–Hafiz

Dad usually came home after a long day running his transportation company. As soon as she heard his key in the door, Mom would rush to the kitchen to put the finishing touches to dinner and get the dishes on the table before he sat down. Us kids waited around the table. Discreetly, we all looked at Dad and listened to the tone of his voice to assess his mood. Was he smiling or frowning?

When Dad was exhausted and frustrated, dinner time could be tense. He had a short fuse and could explode when he felt under pressure. My father was a domineering figure that all of us both loved and feared in equal degrees, Mom included.

But I do not remember many meals in Tehran with my entire family—Mom, Dad, my three siblings and me—around the table. Our family unit did not remain whole for long. The revolution, the repression that followed and the Iran-Iraq war all conspired to blow Iranian families apart. Ours, like countless others, grew smaller as one by one my siblings moved abroad.

We kept in touch, of course, through letters and costly phone conversations across the world, long before email and Internet calls made communications easier. Our sense of family was strong and deeply ingrained. Even if not present physically, my siblings were still part of our lives.

But their departure affected us all. Goodbyes were heartbreaking, Mom stoically fighting tears and trying to focus on the positive— the opportunities she was giving her offspring by letting them go. But inside, her heart was breaking into pieces.

• • •

My eldest sister Niloo was the first to go. I was only 6 years old when she got married at the age of 17 and left to live in America with her Iranian husband who was a student in the US. I never got a chance to get to know her very well, until my own move to the US nearly two decades later.

On her wedding day, I looked up in awe at Niloo's round, beautiful face with her big eyes, long eyelashes, pouty lips and fair skin. She was the spitting image of my mother: Niloo and Mom looked more like sisters than mother and daughter. But then, my mother was only 33 years old at the time.

Looking back now, I wonder how my mom felt about having a married daughter at an age when many women in the Western world are only just thinking of settling down. On Niloo's big day, did Mom reflect on her own wedding at the tender age of 15?

As a six-year-old, I could not tell if Niloo was happy or sad that day. Her mood seemed to shift during the day. She was excited to start a new chapter in a new country, with a husband by her side. But it meant leaping into the unknown and leaving her family behind. Whatever it was, it made my child's heart uneasy. I clung to the bottom of her white wedding dress, followed her around and did not leave her side the entire day, insisting on sitting right next to her. Was it my way of saying, "Don't leave me behind, take me with you!" Or was it a clumsy, childish attempt to protect her? Maybe I was just in awe of this beautiful bride. In her white dress and makeup, my eldest sister looked like a princess, and I could not take my eyes off of her.

A couple of weeks after the wedding, we all assembled at the airport to watch the newlyweds depart. My mom, dad and Roya embraced the young couple with heavy hearts. I held on to Niloo's hand and wept. Seeing the adults cry was upsetting.

My eldest sister, very emotional, stooped down, held me tight in her arms and whispered in my ear:

"Don't cry. I will be back soon, and I will bring you the most beautiful doll I can find".

Had Niloo promised a soccer ball, I might have stopped crying, but the promise of a doll did not comfort me one bit!

.   .   .

I am the youngest of four children—11 years younger than Niloo, 9 years younger than my second sister Roya and 7 years apart from my brother Joseph. As a young child, I did not really connect with any of my siblings because of the substantial age difference. I was the baby in the family, the latecomer who arrived on the scene long after the others.

Although Joseph was closest in age to me, I did not spend much time with him either, even if he did not leave Iran until several years later and I only grew close to my sister Roya during my teenage years, when she was in her twenties and the gap between us had shrunk. My sister became a mother figure in my life, a trusted ally who looked out for me. To this day, Roya and I enjoy a tight bond. She is my confidante, the person I turn to whenever I need support or advice.

.   .   .

When I started school, Roya would take my hand and guide me down the street, very conscious of her big sister role. She took the job of escorting me to my elementary school every morning seriously. I was drowning in the hideous dark school uniform we were forced to wear, a drab Islamic garment much too large for my skinny body. I was only seven, and it looked particularly grim on small kids like me.

Around the time I started primary education, our family moved from our place near downtown Tehran to an apartment that was slightly smaller but in a better location, near one of the city's most beautiful green spaces, Park-e Saie. It was also more conveniently located near my school.

When I woke up every morning, I put on the wide pants and the "manteau" (a term borrowed from the French for coat) that Mom had pressed and laid out in my room the night before.

"Quick, we're going to be late, Naz," Roya urged me as I finished breakfast. On my way out of the door, I picked up my "maghnae", a balaclava-type head covering that ensured no wisp of hair was visible. We kept it by the front door. It made my head itch, and I did not want to wear it a second longer than was strictly necessary. I only put it on as we stepped out of the apartment.

Roya would drop me by the imposing gate. My protective sister always waited and made sure that I was safely inside before turning around and continuing on her way to her high school a couple of blocks away.

Inside the vast courtyard, we all had to stand in line before class. The entire school, from first to fifth grade, assembled every morning. We were all girls: Co-eds were banned after the revolution. We waited for the principal, a mean woman appointed for her allegiance to the regime, to show up. All our teachers were also women. The only men allowed on the premises were the janitor and a security guard who ensured that no students wandered away from the school complex.

"Repeat after me," the principal shouted. "Khomeini, Khomeini, you are light from God." Obediently, we echoed her chants in praise of the Supreme Leader and the ugly attacks against the perceived enemies of the regime. "Death to the Shah", "Death to Imperialism."

In schools all over the country, a similar ritual played out every day. At all levels of education, the country's religious leaders had revised the school curriculum to reflect "Islamic values." It is never too early to start indoctrinating children! All subjects were affected: Centuries of Persian history were erased from history manuals or entirely rewritten to reflect the mullah's thinking.

After attempting to inject revolutionary spirit in our minds with slogans, the principal tried to improve our bodies with jumping jacks and other gymnastic exercises to wake us up and get our blood flowing. Before class even started, we were already hot and sweaty. Try doing gymnastics wearing a coat that reaches below your knees! The manteau restricted our movements, serving its purpose: Girls were meant to behave modestly, not run wild or climb trees.

"Ready, march!" At the end of the session, we all dutifully formed a line, walked to our classroom and sat at our benches, prepared to start our day of learning.

I did not enjoy school. Too many of the subjects we studied struck me as useless. They were boring. The only exciting time was the first day of the academic year when we received new school supplies. Mom bought colorful paper—the kind you use to wrap gifts—and we would cut it down to the right size and create a protective cover to prevent school manuals and notebooks from getting ripped or dirty.

•   •   •

I was on my own a lot as a young child but my active imagination prevented loneliness and alienation. I daydreamed and created stories.

Whirling around the bedroom I shared with Roya, I practiced the graceful arm movements of traditional Iranian dancing. Painting, drawing, dancing, pretend play and other artsy activities kept me busy. I would fill pages of notebooks with elegant Persian script, spending hours improving my calligraphy skills. Around the age of ten, I started writing poetry. Women and girls were not encouraged, or even allowed, to engaged in artistic pursuits in Iran at the time.

From America, Niloo sent us pictures, magazines and home videos that showed a very different lifestyle. As I got older, I became more aware of the restrictions imposed by the regime. My dreams of a life of freedom outside Iran were further stoked by a steady diet of Western movies and television. In my teens, one of my passions was listening to Western pop music—Madonna, Michael Jackson as well as British banks like Culture Club, Pink Floyd and Queen were among my favorites. We grabbed whatever bootleg copies of 80s hits we could get our hands on in the black market.

I also pored over fashion magazines for hours and then tweaked my clothes in an attempt to emulate the styles. One of our neighbors, who lived next door and was considered an "Auntie", imported clothes from Turkey that she sold from her condo. She knew I loved fashion and always gave me first pick of a few items every time she received a shipment. I cherished them! I "distressed" the jeans I wore under my school uniforms, incurring my mom's wrath for messing up my clothes.

Outside of school I wore punk clothes and cultivated just enough of a tough girl attitude to earn the respect of my school mates. I wanted the freedom to express who I was. But the political climate meant that my look and attitude always made me guilty of something. It led to some devastating fights with my parents, who could not understand why I would not conform.

•   •   •

My mother, a small, fragile, soft spoken woman, married my dad when she was only 15. He was 32 years old. The year was 1962 and theirs was an arranged marriage, as many Iranian marriages were at the time. Mom did not even meet her prospective husband until their wedding day. She had grown up with three sisters in a semi-religious family. I cannot imagine how this 15-year-old innocent and sheltered girl felt when she was yanked out of school to become of the wife of a much older man overnight. My maternal grandmother had arranged the union behind closed doors with my dad's mother, who was not a very pleasant woman. My mom never had a say in the matter. She was not just marrying my dad; she was marrying his entire family. As was customary, she would move into their large household, where she was surrounded by complete strangers. My father's siblings and parents made the start of her married life very difficult until the new couple could move into a place of their own.

When I was nine years old , my mother contracted a sudden and mysterious illness that nearly killed her and shook our family to the core. One cold November, when we were on vacation in the north of Iran by the Caspian Sea with family friends, my mom fell violently ill.

Her fever spiked and her situation deteriorated so much that she could barely open her eyes. We rushed back to Tehran and took her straight to the hospital, where she remained for a month. The entire family was in a state of shock.

None of my mother's doctors could figure out what was wrong with her. Her condition continued to worsen and she slipped into a coma. No closer to a diagnosis, the physicians warned us that she might be nearing the end. Niloo rushed back from the US and was there when the doctors told my family to say goodbye and prepare for the worst.

Dad and my relatives felt I was too young to absorb the news that my mother might die, and they wanted to shield me. I will never forget the desperate cries and screams by my mom's bed. My pious grandmother was praying and bargaining with God, begging for a miracle to let her daughter live. My sisters and Joseph were quietly weeping, at a loss for words. Even my dad, who was not a man prone to expressing his feelings, had tears trickling down his face. Despite all the fights and arguments between them, he really loved my mom. I may have been too young to fully understand the gravity of the situation, but I knew it was bad.

My mother was saved thanks to a doctor who passed her hospital room on his way to see another patient. He had noticed my mom, a 37-year-old woman, deathly pale and unconscious on her hospital bed, and breathing through a ventilator while her distraught mother, husband and children cried by her bed. He stopped and asked them about her case, curious about her diagnosis. When my aunt relayed the information provided by my mom's doctor, he asked for permission to examine her. After a brief examination, he yelled at the nurse, "Operating Room, NOW."

My mother had contracted a bacterial disease that ate away at her intestines, leaving a large hole. The infection rapidly spread to the rest of the body, affecting other vital organs. Had the doctor not immediately resected the diseased bowel section, she would not have survived.

My mom still refers to this astute physician, who diagnosed her ailment when his colleagues failed to do so, as her guardian angel. Mom was in no doubt that she had come very close to death. Later, she recalled seeing a bright light and feeling that she was leaving her body. But she was also conscious of her family around her. She heard her mother's prayers, her husband's and children's pleas and fought a little harder to come back to us all.

Shortly after the surgery, my mother emerged from her coma and slowly began to recover, although it took a while until she could leave hospital and resume a normal life.

.   .   .

My father, a tall, imposing man from Hamedan in north-western Iran, was one of ten children. As a kid, I often looked at my paternal grandmother and wondered how in the world that tiny frame of hers managed to give birth to so many large humans. She was a skinny woman with bright blue eyes and fair skin who looked more Eastern European than Iranian. Dad inherited her blue eyes and passed them down to my brother Joseph.

In a world dominated by Eurocentric beauty standards, I was very jealous of my dad and brother's fair eyes and light brown hair color. I thought it was unfair that us girls did not inherit these characteristics. As a beauty-conscious teen, I remember begging Niloo to bring me blue contact lenses from America when she visited us in Tehran and I often asked my mom to let me color my hair lighter. Even in Iranian society, blond hair and blue eyes were considered the epitome of beauty and I knew it opened doors and presented more opportunities. With these attributes, you could become an actor if you so desired, no credentials needed. I dreamed of being in the movies and therefore subscribed to this ideal for a long time.

I still had that picture etched in my head when I moved to the States and traveled throughout America and Europe. The diversity in America opened my eyes to many different versions of beauty and gave me a newfound sense of pride and gratitude for my brown eyes, dark hair and olive skin.

However, I was always curious about the light complexion on my dad's side of family and wanted to know more about our heritage. Years later, Roya decided to have a DNA test. It did not surprise me that, alongside Iranian genes, our genetic material contained a sprinkling of Eastern European genes.

In his last years, when he lived in Southern California, my father would often take long walks and go to a park where he sat on a bench to read his newspaper. Other elderly folks would sometimes sit next to him and strike up a friendly conversation. They were offended when my dad said, "NO English" and assumed he was just an anti-social American man who did not want to talk. They found it hard to believe he was from the Middle East and not a white man.

• • •

As the older son, my father was expected to provide for his parents and siblings as well as his wife and children. It is natural to assume that a man will always prioritize the needs of his wife and children, and Dad did that... to some extent. But he grew up in a collectivist culture and felt obligated to look after his relatives. Trying to keep two households happy was a constant balancing act that caused him enormous stress and often triggered fights with my mothers.

My dad had a very short temper. He had a tough upbringing. Later in life, I learned that in his youth, he accidentally ran over a little boy who had suddenly run onto the road in front of his car, killing the child. My dad pressed on the brake but was unable to stop in time. Road-related car accidents are frequent in Iran, which has one of the highest rates of traffic deaths and injuries in the world, but this tragic episode scarred my dad for life.

Dad was also very old-fashioned and strict, which made life hard for his much younger wife and subsequently for us kids. As the youngest, I was born when Dad was already in his mid-forties. Beyond the generational gap, he represented a patriarchal culture that still prevailed in parts of Iran, even though the country's elites in the fancy parts of Tehran were largely westernized.

My parents had a very intense and unhealthy relationship, and they often fought. The fights between them sometimes turned physical. I grew up witnessing domestic abuse and violent disputes. My sisters tell me tension at home was far worse before I was born or when I was too young to remember. Exposed to a violent relationship at a young age, I assumed it was the way marriages functioned. This had a lasting impact on my life and might explain why I got involved in dysfunctional relationships as an adult.

Most arguments revolved around two things: Money and my dad's family. Occasionally, they centered on my brother or me since we were the two troublemakers in the family.

The only difference was that my mom always had a special place in her heart for Joseph, her only son. She always defended him, shielding him at all costs from my dad's anger and disapproval.

Dad had a soft spot for me, his youngest, his baby girl and he indulged me when I was a young kid. But his attitude began to shift when I hit adolescence and shed my tomboy image. As I spent more time with my girlfriends, became interested in boys and started experimenting with makeup and trendy clothes, those changes did not sit well with my father and caused an enormous amount of friction between us. Dad and I had vastly different perspectives on life and we lost our connection.

I had a natural tendency to question authority but, paradoxically, it was also influenced by my dad's outspoken nature. In many ways, Dad was the one who planted the seeds of rebellion in me. From a very early age, I heard him rant about the regime. He was very open about his opposition to the mullahs and frequently discussed political developments with friends and with members of our enlarged family who spent a lot of time at our home.

Like clockwork, he watched the news on TV every evening, a habit I picked up from him and maintain to this day. Every day, Dad read the newspaper cover to cover, his face disappearing for long periods behind the pages stretched between his two hands. Once he was done with one page, he passed it on to me to catch up on the latest news. Like my dad, I wanted to know what was going on, but what filtered out also fueled the growing sense of injustice that boiled inside me.

At home, us kids never discussed our goals and ambitions with our parents. Looking back, I wonder if my mom, my dad ever harbored dreams of their own when they were young. If they did, they never let on. Given the hostile environment we lived in under the regime, they wanted us to keep our heads down, obey the rules, and avoid being too ambitious or getting into trouble.

My parents had no idea what I wanted to do with my life, what my passions were. They never showed an interest or asked, so I never shared! In any case, if I had told them about my artistic aspirations, they would have discouraged me.

Their plan for me was that I would graduate high school, get married, and then live a quiet life. But I was not interested in cooking or cleaning house. After all my siblings moved to the US, they thought I might follow them after graduating high school. I wanted to forge my own path rather than conform to social expectations. I was a natural-born rebel and wanted a lot more. I had big dreams!

.   .   .

As a young child, I liked to be outside. You could find me playing soccer, hopscotch or building a snowman... until THAT day.

One afternoon I ran home, horrified, after making up some excuse and leaving my position in the middle of a soccer match. I had just spotted blood on my pants, in the crotch area, and thought I had an incurable disease and was dying.

My mother had never warned me about the unexpected guest that visits young women once they hit puberty. Even with girls and boys attending separate schools, anatomy, sex education and other sensitive topics were never covered in class. They were not considered appropriate. Nor were they discussed much in the privacy of our home or in the wider society. They remained largely taboo. Preparing us for puberty was deliberately ignored. Instead of learning about our bodies and their natural functions, we were forced to study the Quran, and we learned to read and write Arabic—mandatory subjects that we all found pointless and uninteresting. Sex ed would have been more useful.

So yes, that day, when I saw blood on my pants, I rushed home, frightened. I hurried into the bathroom and slammed the door behind me. My mom noticed the terror in my eyes as I ran past her and could tell something was not right. She came knocking on the bathroom door worried that something serious had happened.

When I tearfully told her that I was probably going to die soon because I was bleeding, she sat me down and we had THE conversation. I was much relieved to hear that death was not imminent and spent the rest of the day at home processing the information provided during this impromptu crash course. Apparently, I had entered womanhood, which signaled the end of the days when I could play outside as a carefree child.

But I felt way too young to act like an adult and I was not ready yet to give up my childhood freedoms. Sadly, change was inevitable and it was time to grow up.

•   •   •

When my parents were not arguing about family matters, they bickered over money struggles. In my early childhood, my dad owned and operated an independent ground transportation company and he made a decent living from transportation. We were not rich by any means, but we were not poor either. We lived comfortably.

I was too young to pay attention to my family's income at the time. Dad worked very hard and came home tired, but with his pockets stuffed full of cash. Investing in gold is a traditional way of saving in the Middle East and my mother's wrists were always adorned with more gold bangles than I could count.

Sadly, these prosperous days came to an end after my dad opted to sell the business and invest instead in a textile factory owned by a friend, who convinced him he would make more money without having to work such long and grueling hours.

It was an enticing offer. Dad was in his 50s at the time and he had worked tirelessly since he was a very young boy. He saw it as an opportunity to ease up and lighten his load. After selling the business he had built from the ground up, he handed all the proceeds of the sale over to his associate.

Unfortunately, the Iraqi air force destroyed their plans. A short while after my father invested in the factory, the building was hit by a rocket that demolished it entirely.

My dad had poured most of the family assets into this venture and we were left with limited savings in the bank. Seeing his life work destroyed also impacted my father mentally: He never found the strength or the will to start another business.

His depressed state created further tensions at home. Mom felt that my dad has given up too easily and she blamed him for handing the family assets over to his friend. Her nagging angered my dad, a proud man who took his responsibility as a provider very seriously. Neither he nor his associate could not have foreseen that the war with Iraq would destroy their livelihood.

•   •   •

One night when I was around 12 or 13 , we were sitting down around the kitchen table for dinner when my parents started arguing again. The argument got very heated. Suddenly my father grabbed the serving dish filled with hot food and threw it at the wall behind my mother's seat. The dish shattered, raining hot food and glass shards all over the place.

Of all their fights, that one stuck with me because I saw the fear in everyone's eyes. My father was a strong and tough man. When my mom bickered and complained at length, I could see that her jabs were hurting his pride and ego and knew that his rage would soon erupt. Mom wanted Dad to put us, his children, first and she wanted a more secure life for us all, and I could not blame her. It broke her heart that after the collapse of Dad's business venture, Roya, who was the most academically gifted of her children and a very successful students, had to give up her hopes of pursuing higher education. Roya was accepted at college but could not attend due to lack of money. It was always her ambition to go to university and get her degree. She did eventually achieve her goal—many years later when she was in her 30s, after she settled in Southern California.

•   •   •

Numerous uncles, aunts and cousins populated our familiar universe as I was growing up. We visited each other and gathered for celebrations. My sisters, being older, were lucky to grow up with their cousins who were of similar age, but I was the baby of the family and did not have playmates during family gatherings.

As children, we awaited the Iranian New Year, Nowruz, with the same excitement American kids look forward to Christmas. The holiday, which marks the beginning of spring, meant 13 days of vacation, family visits and receiving cash from the older family members as a gift, as younger members of the large family paid their respects to their elders.

We started preparing for Nowruz weeks ahead of the event. First step: Spring cleaning. We went through every drawer, cabinet and window to ensure that everything was tidy and sparkled. The process took days. Then we watered seeds and left them in a dish to sprout so we would have green shoots to display among the seven items that symbolize renewal. These also included boiled and painted eggs that we enjoyed making, while Mom got busy in the kitchen and prepared various traditional dishes.

On the 13th day, families spent the day outdoors on picnics—a bonus for burglars who found many homes empty. In my early childhood, I remember fun outings with uncles, aunts and cousins. Each family had a car and we drove to rural areas an hour or two away from the city. We favored a beautiful picnic spot near Karaj, located by a river. My mom and the other women in the family brought food and snacks. The adults chatted while the kids ran wild. Memories of these festive early Nowruz are still vivid in my memory.

Over the years, the impact of the war and the economic downturn began to take their toll. Nowruz was still celebrated, but it was more restrained and felt less festive. I still enjoyed Charshanbe Soori, the last Tuesday evening of our year, just before Nowruz, when old and young leapt over a bonfire. The ancient ritual helped us get rid of the sadness and sorrows of the past year and allowed us to start the new one unburdened. We screamed and laughed as we jumped over the flames, experiencing the same mix of terror and delight you feel on a vertiginous rollercoaster ride.

The radical clerics who ran our country frowned upon Nowruz and its attended symbolisms, left over from Iran's pre-Islamic culture. But the Persian new year is one of our oldest and most sacred traditions, practiced by Persians for thousands of years, and they never dared to ban it entirely, knowing it would cause inevitable popular outrage. But they did their best to dampen our fun: When the celebrations coincide with religious events, such as the fasting month of Ramadan, which is based on the lunar calendar and therefore happens at a different time each year, rules were stricter and no public signs of joy were allowed.----

When financial pressure grew and Dad felt weighed down by his role as provider for two households, he took out his anger and frustration on my mom and sometimes my siblings. As I got older, I began to understand the cycle of abuse and the pain that my mother had endured.

Although my relationship with my mom did not progress much significantly until a couple of decades later, when I was in my 30s, I gradually understood the struggles that had shaped her and made her the way she was.

I often felt emotionally neglected and ignored as a child. In the eyes of the child that I was, my mom often appeared detached and uninterested, although she always tended to all our physical needs. We were fed nutritious and delicious food. The house was always clean and we were well clothed. She had a stronger connection with my older siblings, and I longed for the same connection and more affection from her, tender gestures and praise, and these were not part of her repertoire. I learned much later that Mom was unaware of my feelings and the hurt that her detachment was causing me at the time. She never intended to hurt or sadden me.

Among friends and relatives, she was known as a kind, caring person—a timid woman who rarely stood up for her own rights. To make sense of our relationship, I had to become more mature and try harder to understand her better. Now I realize that she fought her own battles, repressing her own pain and suffering for years. Struggling to make it through the battles of daily life, she was wrung dry and had little emotional support to offer her youngest daughter.

Learning more about Mom's tough life made me realize how strong and resilient she was, and still is. Her husband was a hard worker who had a strong sense of his responsibilities toward his family. But he was also demanding, quarrelsome and never lifted a finger to help in the household. The responsibility of looking after their four children fell squarely on my mother's shoulders.

In spite of the difficulties she faced, she still found a way to forgive and remain kind and gracious. After going through my fair share of tough moments in my childhood and youth, I managed to overcome hardship with my head held high. I chose to become a survivor rather than a victim.

I doubt I would have found the strength and decency to forgive my abusers and not seek revenge the way that my mom had. I still feel sad for that little girl who yearned so desperately for her mother's love and affection, but I now know that I get my patience, grace and resilience from my mother.

Now that I understand my mom's struggles better, I marvel that after all she has gone through, she is still standing strong, proud and poised. I have no doubt that my mother is the reason I am here today. It was not obvious to me for a long time, but it is now perfectly clear where I got the fighter in me.

CHAPTER THREE

Guardian Angel

"Anyone who genuinely and consistently with both hands
looks for something, will find it."
–Rumi

y the age of 20, my brother Joseph could not afford to push his luck any further after getting into trouble on several occasions with the morality police. My parents, fearing for his life, sold their valuable possessions to raise enough money and get him out of Iran. By then, many of our friends and relatives had already left the country.

I remember that my mother's arms, with their porcelain skin, looked bare without the jingling gold bangles that my dad had bought her over the years. The handwoven silk Persian rug in our living-room was replaced with a cheaper version and my parents dug into whatever was left of the family savings to procure a passport for Joseph by bribing a civil servant in the passport office.

Joseph was a fun-loving teenager who enjoyed the lighter side of life. He partied, enjoyed drinking and hanging out with friends, including girls. In that, he was no different from his peers in Western countries where such behavior would have been considered normal, even tame.

But in Iran, anything that was not related to Islamic religion was considered a crime and prohibited. In effect, the authorities had banned joy! Speaking verses from the Holy Koran was the only form of "entertainment" officially allowed. Hanging out with members of the opposite sex was, of course, an absolute no-no unless they were direct relatives—husband, dad or brother.

The religious militias that patrolled our neighborhood had party-going Joseph in their sights, waiting for him to commit another misstep so they could take him in to custody again. It was just a matter of time. After the brutal flogging he had experienced, he risked further beatings or being sent to a dark detention center from which he might not emerge.

The ongoing Iran-Iraq war gave efforts to get Joseph out of the country added urgency as the pointless murder of conscripts continued. Like all young men, my brother could be drafted into the army at short notice. Serving was mandatory and since Joseph had not yet contributed to the war effort—as the authorities saw it— he was not allowed to leave the country. Paying a corrupt official was the only way.

As casualties soared, Mom could not sleep at night. She did not want to lose her only son to a senseless war, fighting for a regime that showed no respect for its people and their wellbeing. So many families had received bad news from the front that the human cost of the conflict was apparent to all, even if the authorities tried hard to keep a lid on casualty figures. The conflict ended up killing up to one million of our compatriots, we learned years later.

Using their contacts and ingenuity, and with a large dose of luck, my parents managed to send my brother to Germany. They secured him a work visa thanks to support from a cousin living there who vouched that my brother would be employed by their company. Joseph lived in Germany for a while before joining our sister Niloo in Southern California.

Our homeland was no longer safe for my brother and he never came back. Nearly a decade went by until I saw him again. Niloo, on the other hand, visited us once or twice a year and entertained us with tales of life in the United States. Her stories provided a glimpse of a world where daily life was not dominated by fear and conflict.

. . .

Mom was very protective of Joseph and harbored a lot of resentment towards my dad's family because of an incident that took place early on in her marriage, when she was pregnant with my brother. The episode illustrates the darker side of large families where rivalries and power struggles are frequent. I only learned about it as an adult and it shocked me.

The main culprit was my aunt Sami, who I had always viewed as my coolest aunt. Following a dispute between my mom and some of Dad's sisters, Sami wanted to make a show of force and demonstrate who was in charge. She teamed up with two of her older sisters to conduct a premeditated, brutal assault on my pregnant mom, kicking her in the stomach. I broke into tears when Mom told me how she was unable to protect her unborn baby, Joseph, who suffered permanent nerve damage to his face as a result of the attack, because Dad's two other sisters held her down to prevent her from fighting back or defending herself. The story broke my heart and I struggled to comprehend that family members could be capable of such evil.

My aunts, who were still living with their parents at the time, carried out the beating while my dad was away on a work trip. Knowing how mean my paternal grandmother often was towards my mom, I suspect she was behind this incident.

My dad did very little to discipline his sisters. Concerned that the situation would escalating further, my mom probably told him to avoid retaliation. The traumatic incident soured my mom's relations with her in-laws. It also caused lasting damage to Joseph.

When Joseph turned 4 or 5, Mom took him to see many doctors, hoping for a miracle. Fearful that he would get bullied at school for his uneven face, she was desperate to find someone who could correct the damaged nerves. One doctor suggested invasive electric shock therapy as a way to re-activate the damaged nerves on young Joseph's numb face, but he turned out to be a charlatan peddling false hopes. Poor Joseph endured several sessions of shock treatment but the painful treatments did more harm than good to Joseph and the mental impact lasts to this day. My mother tried everything in her power to mitigate the consequences of this atrocity committed by relatives on an innocent child still in utero. Somehow, she felt guilty and responsible, although none of it was her fault. Joseph's big green eyes and light brown hair made him stand out, but his crooked smile made him look different from other kids.

This was not the only time Mom was ill-treated by her in-laws. Dad's mother never showed her an ounce of warmth when she joined the family, a child bride yanked away from her own parents at a tender age. On occasions, my grandmother locked Mom up in the basement of their house, leaving her in the cold, damp and dark underground vault without any food or water. This extreme cruelty was unusual, but in many traditional societies, in the Middle East and elsewhere around the world, young brides entering a new family were at times abused and exploited. I would learn the hard way that even in the middle class, mistreatment of daughters-in-law is not uncommon.

An extended family can be a complex, hierarchical structure riven with rivalries and jealousies. But large families are also sources of support and fun. We spent a lot of time with relatives as children and gatherings that involved uncles, aunts and cousins were among the highlights of my Iranian childhood. As I experienced on several occasions, at its best, an extended family involves sharing and solidarity, and provides a safety net during periods of hardship.

I didn't know my paternal grandparents well, but I remember that my dad's father was nicer than his wife. He showed us grandkids some affection, unlike his wife who was cold and unlikable. Grandpa was a big, tall man who was bald, fat and usually quiet. A great poet, he was also very eccentric and believed in fairies. He had a passion for cats and was convinced he could understand them.

When I was around 14 years old, the foundation of the four-story apartment block we lived in started to crack. The walls were splitting open, and the building was in danger of collapsing.

We packed up what we could and left in a hurry before it collapsed and buried us. While repairs were conducted and our home was made safe for habitation again, we stayed with my grandparents. Most kids look forward to spending time being pampered and spoiled by loving grandparents, but our stay was not pleasant. My formidable grandmother was not the warm, affectionate kind. Both of my dad's parents passed away not long after we returned to our own home.

· · ·

After Joseph left in the late 1980s, Roya and I were the only siblings left in Iran. By then in my teens, I was old enough to develop a meaningful relationship with my sister who was in her early twenties. I looked up to her. In spite of the nine-year age difference, we enjoyed chatting and doing things together.

Always a hard-worker, Roya had found a great job at IBM and was rapidly moving up in the company. A fighter, she was kind and fiercely protective of her little sister. In sharp contrast with my more traditional parents, she was a progressive and independent thinker, rejecting social expectations. Like me, she wanted to make her own choices.

In the eyes of the teenage rebel that I was, Roya symbolized cool. She proved a valuable ally when I overstepped the boundaries set by my parents and society. When I needed my mom and she did not show up for me, Roya had my back.

With two of their four children now living in the States, my parents were spending more time across the Atlantic. Niloo was starting a family and my brother was settling down. Mom and Dad would spend a month or two at a time in California, helping them both get situated.

In their absence, Roya was asked to look after me. As we navigated life together while our parents were gone, my bond with Roya grew stronger. I listened to her every word, watched her interact with people, studied how she dressed, and admired how she carried herself and handled different situations. I would absorb all aspects of her, including her chosen hobbies: She was my role model and I wanted to be just like her.

My admiration for her did not prevent occasional disputes. We were siblings, after all, and indulged in mild rivalries. But mostly, I looked forward to these periods alone with her when home rules were relaxed. We had fun!

.   .   .

Closer in age to me than my parents and more open-minded, Roya understood the deep-seated sense of anger and helplessness that fueled my defiance. She shared some of my feelings but controlled them better. As a child, I never accepted what I was told unless it made sense to me: I needed logic and explanations to form my own opinion. I wanted to do things my own way.

Inquisitiveness is normally viewed as a positive characteristic in a child, but my curious mind did not work in my favor in a country controlled by religious extremists. The government insisted that the strict rules enforced by the morality police were guided by Sharia law, and therefore dictated by Allah himself. This was not a place for an independent thinker who questioned every rule and wanted to know the why and how. As I grew older and more confident, this became evident.

I wanted to express my creativity but the dress code prevented any show of individuality. Women were not allowed to paint their nails and show their hair. We could be stopped in the street if strands of hair fell out from under our hijab. Showing any skin was considered seductive, so every inch of our body—apart from the face and hands—had to be hidden.

The Morality Squads were meant to intimidate us and force us into submission. These were the same men, dressed in olive drab uniforms like combat soldiers, who had targeted and beaten my brother. Now it was my turn.

One day I was walking to a friend's house, a block down the road when I ran into a boy from my neighborhood. We stopped and chatted about music—we both enjoyed Michael Jackson's newest album—and decided to trade cassette tapes of the latest hits in western pop music. I don't know how I could have missed the Morality Police following us around our block. As the boy and I were exchanging our cassettes discretely the way drug dealers slip the goods into their customer's hand, I felt a sharp jab between my shoulder blades. It was the barrel of a rifle. Next thing we knew we were handcuffed and thrown into the back of a car. From a distance, they had spotted two kids of the opposite sex chatting animatedly and exchanging something suspicious.

When we got to the station— a forbidding, bunker-like building surrounded by barbed wire—I was locked up in a holding cell like a common criminal in the company of a few women who might have been sex workers while my friend was taken to the male section. Remembering the blood that soaked through my brother's shirt after he was flogged, I was crying and shaking with fear. Who knew what these stern and fanatical men would do to me? I was also terrified of my dad's reaction. I was 13 years old.

Crouched in a corner of the cold cell, away from the others, I cried silently. After a couple hours that went on forever, a guard escorted me out of the room. They had contacted my dad who was there to pick me up.

My father's face was red with fury when I appeared. Dad no longer saw me as his innocent little girl. Since I had reached puberty, I had become a problem. At that moment, I honestly didn't know which was scarier: Facing my dad or being kept in that depressing jail cell? For me, it was a lose-lose situation.

Dad was forced to bribe the morality police and beg them to overlook the behavior of his "stupid little girl who did not know what she was doing."

But he was wrong. I knew exactly what I was doing: I could not accept rules that prevented me from talking to a friend in broad daylight—so what, if he's a boy? Nor did I understand why listening to music was such a crime if other children around the world were free to do so. My only regret was that I got caught and my family had to pay these disgusting creatures and beg them for mercy. But I was not sorry for wanting a sense of normalcy in my life.

I hoped my mother would deflect my father's anger when we got home and shield me the way she had protected Joseph. But she let me down. Far from accepting that I had done nothing wrong, she ganged up with my dad, blaming me for being a troublemaker.

I was at the beginning of a period of teenage rebellion and once more, I was found guilty before even being given a hearing.

This episode amplified my frustration. It was not fair that kids couldn't enjoy themselves and engage in innocent and wholesome activities. Why did our government give these parasites the authority to treat us children like criminals? All we wanted was a normal life and a bit of fun. Listening to music was not a crime and I should not have risked arrest and imprisonment.

I became a contrarian, refusing to bend to the wills of my teachers, my parents and my leaders. If I was going to be accused whether or not I had done anything wrong, I figured I might as well do the deeds.

This incident marked a turning point in my young life. I had been asking questions, trying to understand the reasons behind the rules. Now I rejected them, and everything my parents, my teachers, my government and all forms of organized religions had taught me.

Doubting or questioning what you were told was not acceptable—neither for the authorities, nor within the family. I was not suited to live in a country where thinking for yourself is considered dangerous and unacceptable. My attitude was causing problems that would only grow as I got older.

·   ·   ·

I often felt that my mother made it a habit to pick on me when I was a child, always blaming me when things went wrong before hearing me out. I grew up feeling that I was always guilty—of something, even if I didn't know what—and had to apologize for my very existence. Maybe it was the duty of the youngest child to carry that burden to maintain the dignity of older children. I was particularly sensitive to criticism from my mother because I felt unseen by her. Maybe she thought that was the only way to tame my rebellious nature, discipline my defiance and keep me out of trouble. Whatever the reason, this perception hurt me deeply and I carried the trauma into adulthood.

It took me decades to understand my mom better. Now I try to imagine what it must have been like to get married at 15 to a man much older, have a first daughter at 16, followed by two more children at two years interval. She probably thought her family was complete by the time I appeared on the scene, seven years after my brother.

With four children and a traditional husband, who worked all hours and never helped at home—on the contrary, he expected to be served—she must have felt overwhelmed. Somewhat unfairly, I placed the bar for my mom far higher than I did for Dad, who was a more absent, though dominant figure.

Until I was in middle school, I was a fairly good student, even if not very academic. But my grades began to slip as I moved into adolescence, and conflict with my parents grew more frequent. I sought solace in pop and rock-pop music— from Pink Floyd to Queen and even Barbra Streisand, and Duran Duran my range was broad. I brought my favorite pop stars into my room, earning my parents' disapproval for sticking posters above my bed. Wearing punk clothes, I developed a defiant attitude to escape the reality that consumed my life.

I was going out more with my close friends Mona, who lived in our neighborhood, and Aram, another close friend from school. During early adolescence, I spent a lot of time at Mona's place. Unlike my conservative parents, hers were progressive and cool—her dad was a university professor. Her cool mom fascinated me and I watched with more than a hint of envy as mother and daughter joked together, exchanged complicit glances and ruffled each other's hair in obvious displays of affection. "If I could be as close to my mom," I thought.

· · ·

I never experienced the same closeness or familiarity with my mother. I was too young at the time to understand that she had not chosen her life any more than I felt free to choose mine. From my perspective, an invisible barrier created distance between us. I never felt close or comfortable enough to open up to her, confide whatever was troubling me as I grew up or ask for motherly advice. If I needed help, Roya was the one I turned to. Unlike me, she got on well with Mom and I was often jealous of their intimacy.

With hindsight, I can see that my parents cared deeply for us, but affectionate gestures were rare and verbal expressions of love rarer still. No daily cuddles and kisses! No I love you's. It was not their style. Mom and Dad were old-fashioned— working hard was their way of loving us. My dad toiled all hours to provide for his family while Mom's main responsibility was to keep us well fed, clothed and healthy. At breakfast, lunch and dinner every day, she expressed her love through the delicious meals she cooked for us. She was an attentive mother: When we got sick, she would prepare special food, juice and homemade remedies and nurse us back to health. After school or when I played outside with my friends in the summer heat, she would hand me my favorite smoothie or shake.

It would take me years to learn that love comes in different forms. My mother's often harsh attitude stemmed partly from a desire to keep me out of trouble and prepare me to operate in a society that was not kind to women. At the time, I did not understand any of this. I yearned for tenderness and affection and what Mom could offer felt short of what I needed.

. . .

When I reached middle school, talking about boys, latest trends and gossiping became far more alluring than attending class. I resented having to chant slogans praising the Supreme Leader who was making my life hell and I hated our uniforms—I defied the rules by pulling my headscarf back to let my bangs show. I barely passed the religion course because I refused to read the Koran. On the other hand, I had perfect grades in English and art, which were my favorite subjects in school. Learning English well was a crucial element of my plan to, maybe one day, join my siblings in the United States. I excelled at sports and physical education. Exerting myself running track in the school courtyard, playing with the volleyball team or, in my teens, whizzing down the ski slopes, became a way of releasing the pent-up negative energy festering inside me. Playing soccer with the neighborhood kids had developed my athletic skills—I beat most of my classmates at sprint and became a valuable player in the high school volleyball team.

Bored out of my mind during a religion class, during my first year of high school, I started doodling one day and drew devil horns on a portrait of Ayatollah Khomeini, the country's highest-ranking mullah. Since I was in first grade, the Supreme Leader had stared at me from the first page of all my textbooks. I was sick of seeing him everywhere. Unfortunately, I was caught defacing him, thus committing an unforgivable crime in the eyes of the school principal and the authorities. In other circumstances, this would at most have called for detention in class. Instead, it turned into a major crisis.

My mom was called into school. She turned pale when she heard what I had done. I could see the horror sink in as she grasped the severity of my offense. She started crying, begging the principal to forgive me for my ignorance. "She is a silly girl who did not understand what she was doing," she pleaded. "She meant no disrespect to the Ayatollah."

Wrong! Once again, a parent was making excuses and speaking on my behalf, when I HAD intended disrespect. Who could blame me? I hated that man for dictating our every move and forcing his version of Islam as a means of control. Who was he to say that his was the right way? I hated his face, his turban and the evil look of his deep set, sunken eyes.

My mother's heart wrenching pleas and copious tears mollified the principal. He took pity on her and agreed not to report me to the authorities. Instead, he imposed a week of suspension from school. My mom was obviously relieved: had my case been referred to the authorities, I could have been imprisoned as an anti-government activist, a traitor and enemy of the Islamic Republic—my fate... unknown.

Mom avoided even looking at me on the way back. Once safely at home, she raised hell, furious that I needed to be bailed out once again. Her anger did not abate for over a week—living under the same roof was not easy during this period when she barely acknowledged my presence at home. I was too immature at the time to see that, for all her faults, she was trying to protect me from a ruthless system that could have destroyed me.

•   •   •

My troubles in school were not over yet. A couple of years later, I got into a physical altercation with another high school student called Maryam who was actually a friend of mine. I cannot even remember what triggered it: Gossip and rumors were constantly swirling around our all-girl school, causing drama. That day, I was passing by a flight of stairs when Maryam launched herself at me from the top of the staircase.

Caught off guard, I pushed her away and tried to defend myself. With my long nails, I ended up scratching her face deeply, drawing some blood.

Other students had witnessed the incident and knew I had not initiated the fight. Maryam and I were both taken to the office of the principal, who called my mom. My rebellious nature had drawn her attention and she disliked me, seeing me as a rabble rouser.

As soon as my mom arrived, I told her the story before she could hear the official version. "Mrs. Meknat, it was not Naz's fault," my friends explained. "We saw the whole thing. She did not start the fight."

But they failed to defuse her anger. I was becoming an embarrassment. Mom was fed up with being called by the principal on a regular basis to account for a daughter who never listened and refused to obey. When the school authorities didn't complain about my defiance, they flagged my bad grades in Arabic and religion. I could not care less about these two subjects.

Mom could no longer take it. She erupted like a volcano, yelling at me in front of the principal, Maryam, her parents and my teachers. "You are trouble," she screamed. "What have I done to deserve a troublemaking daughter like you?"

I begged Mom to listen, explaining that I had not started the fight, but I could not stop her. Maryam's parents, on the other hand, had chosen to support their daughters. They hugged her and examined the scratch on her face with concern. I desperately wanted my mother to listen to my explanations before jumping to the conclusion that I was to blame, for once. To no avail. Even if I was innocent this time, my reputation as a rebel was already well established in her mind and in the eyes of the principal. My claim of innocence fell on deaf ears: to my mom, I was the "girl who cried wolf."

At this moment, I wanted the earth to swallow me up. I, too, was embarrassed—not for what I had done, but for my mother's very public vote of no confidence in me. I wanted her to come to my defense and fight for me, but my lioness of a mother was not on my side. Maryam and I both got suspended for a week. Fun fact, decades later, we are still friends, although she lives on the other side of the world.

The rant continued when we got home. I knew I was not the easiest or most obedient of teenagers, but I expect my parents—my mother in particular—to cut me some slack. We lived in extraordinary circumstances. I was far from perfect, but I was not the rotten apple my parents made me to be.

Adolescence is a period of turmoil for most adolescents. Navigating hormonal surges and heightened emotions while living in a fishbowl, under constant scrutiny of an authoritarian regime was hard. I needed space to express myself. Most importantly, I needed my mother to listen to my woes, understand what I was going through, and give me a chance before assuming the worst.

That day, I hit a new low. I even felt unwelcome in my own home where the atmosphere crackled with tension after my all-out fight with Mom. I craved her love and affection but failed to get her attention.

I had been wrongly accused before, but this time it hit me hard. My heart was hurting. With nowhere to turn to, I fell into a dark hole. Enough, I was done! Clearly, my existence was just a burden for my parents. If my mom could not show concern for her CHILD who had just been physically assaulted at school, when would she? Angst and dark feelings swelled inside me. I felt defeated and misunderstood.

I knew that my mom kept some pills in her nightstand drawer. As expected, I found a bottle of Valium, still full. At that moment, life did not feel worth living. Feelings of unworthiness, pain, shame and loneliness overwhelmed me. Returning to the bedroom I shared with Roya, I emptied the bottle and ingested all the pills at once washing them down with a glass of water. Then I lied down on my bed and stared at the ceiling while drifting into a deep sleep. I hope never to wake up.

A few years earlier, a friend of mine had taken her own life. I often thought of her and the unbearable pain, isolation and sense of abandonment she must have felt to opt for such a drastic measure. That day, I felt her suffering and thought I wanted the same release. The almighty row with my mom justified my action, according to my young teenage mind.

I don't know how much time passed until Roya came home from work. She walked into the bedroom and found me in deep torpor, breathing slowly and heavily. Something was not right. "Mom!", She called, walking out of the room. "Why is Naz asleep at this hour? She never takes naps. Is she ill?"

"I don't know. She got in trouble at school again and got suspended for a week," Mom told her. "We fought earlier and she got upset."

Roya attempted to wake me up, calling my name repeatedly. No reaction! Then, she tried to shake my limp body, but again got no response. Suddenly, she spotted the empty bottle of Valium on the nightstand between our beds and started screaming. "MOM! Call an ambulance.!

I remember waking up in the shower, looking up and seeing Roya's tear-streamed face. Two paramedics, one on each side, were trying to hold me up. I had a tube down my throat and they were pumping my stomach.

Days later, I heard that, according to the paramedics, I escaped death by a matter of minutes. Had Roya come home a little later that day and not found me when she did, I would not be here today. Thanks to Roya, my rock, my own guardian angel, I had a lucky escape.

CHAPTER FOUR

BEAUTIFUL BOXER

"Reason is powerless in the expression of love."
–Rumi

Hurry," Dad called, urgently. "We must leave now." It was Friday, the Iranian weekend, and we had just sat down for dinner when the sirens started shrieking across the city, emitting a blood-curdling sound to warn us of imminent air raids.

Grabbing a blanket each, Mom, Dad, Roya and I ran across the street to seek protection in the basement of the high-rise building opposite our apartment block. By now, we knew the drill. We raced down to the vast basement where dozens of building residents and people from the neighborhood sat under dim lighting, looking slightly dazed.

Constructed with giant steel columns and superior quality concrete, the building was, we believed, strong enough to withstand the bombs and rockets that were raining down from the sky.

Sirens frequently blared during what became known as the War of the Cities, when Tehran and other major urban centers were directly targeted. The conflict between Iran and Iraq had raged since the beginning of the 1980s and spilled beyond the border regions. Detonations, followed by plumes of dust and smoke rising above impact sites, became part of daily life in the capital. Terrified, we sought shelter underground and hoped for the best.

"Naz, over here," I turned around and was relieved to see Pooneh, one of my best friends who lived on the 15th floor of that building, one of the nicest residential blocks in the area. The shrill sound of the sirens and the distant rumble of explosions set my nerves on edge. It was nice to see a friendly face. I signaled to my parents that I was going to join my friend and sat with Pooneh at one end of the basement. Her parents were chatting with neighbors and paid us no attention.

For the next couple of hours, until the all-clear sounded and we could all return home, Pooneh and I indulged in school gossip and light banter like normal 14-year-old girls—anything that would distract us from the death and destruction above our heads.

It was in that grim setting that I first noticed Pooneh's brother Hamid, who was four years my senior. That's a big age gap when you are a kid. He had been a figure in the background so far, but I was now a teenager and Hamid struck me as an interesting guy, self-confident and outgoing. I had plenty of opportunity to spend time with Pooneh and her brother during these forced visits to the shelter, courtesy of the Iraqi air force. The most intense round of raids on cities that we had experienced were unleashed by Iraq when it began using a new long-range missile targeting major cities, killing more than 400 civilians, injuring many more and causing widespread damage in urban centers. It was terrifying!

The daily alerts took their toll: We were all nervous wrecks, weary of a war that seemed endless. Although we did not know it at the time, these air assaults on the city would be the last. A ceasefire was declared in August that year, putting an end to eight years of conflict and bloodshed.

In the shelter, Hamid still saw me as his kid sister's friend but he was kindly and occasionally chatted with us. It took another couple of years until we got to know each other better and our relationship evolved into something different.

• • •

As I got older and started going out more with a group of friends, I crossed paths with Hamid on numerous occasions. He and his friends sometimes joined our little cohort meeting wherever we could without attracting the attention of the morality police. Pooneh, in awe of her big brother, mentioned that he had a girlfriend who was adored by his family. We all attended parties thrown by friends who had more liberal parents and met up in coffee shops, where we would sit separately from the boys in an adjacent table, pretending we are not together in case the morality police came around. Most of the time, we gathered in the spacious inner courtyard of Pooneh and Hamid's high-rise apartment building, which shielded us from prying eyes. Over time, it became our favorite hangout—a second home to many of us.

Pooneh and Hamid's father died of a sudden heart attack at the age of 49 when I was 16. Both his children were understandably in shock. In Iran, when a family member died, we mourned their loss for forty days straight, wearing nothing but black clothing. You could say that post-revolution, our culture celebrated the dead more than the living, maybe as a side-effect of the regime that made grief more acceptable than celebration. After the revolution, most of Iran's national holidays were religious ones. The mullahs expected us to mourn the anniversary of Prophet Mohammad's death or that of one of the Imams who succeeded him, and they tried to do away with secular holidays, though they had to draw the line at Nowruz, the New Day that marks the start of the Persian new year, celebrated for thousands of years, for fear of triggering a popular backlash.

People dropped by Pooneh and Hamid's place to offer support to the bereaved family. I spent most of my days there, trying to be a kind and supportive friend. Hamid and I established a connection during this period and we started to have feelings for one another. This took us both by surprise, coming out of the blue! We did not speak about it, but we were both aware of what was happening.

•   •   •

A few months later, when the mourning period was over, on a warm summer night, the three of us and two other friends were driving to an underground party. Normal life was slowly returning for Hamid and Pooneh after the tragic loss of their dad. The two of them were sitting with me on the back seat of a friend's car. Hamid was sitting in the middle, squeezed between his sister and me. With the windows rolled up to block out the sound, the five of us were joking, laughing and loudly singing the lyrics of the pop songs.

All of a sudden, Hamid's hand lightly touched mine. I felt struck by a thunderbolt! Caught by surprise, I pulled my hand away. Unfazed, Hamid gently grabbed it again and looked at me. As his hazel eyes drilled into mine, a warm fuzzy feeling spread through my body. Transfixed, I felt butterflies in my stomach.

This was a first for me: I had never had a boyfriend or been with a man before. I glanced at Pooneh to see if she had noticed but she was looking out of the window, not paying attention. I relaxed and allowed myself to be swept by the sensation of Hamid's warm hand on mine. I was falling in love!

Hamid was still seeing his girlfriend and they were expected to announce their engagement any day, Pooneh had told me with great excitement. Their mother, Parvin, had engineered the match. She wanted her only son to marry a girl from a wealthy, prominent family. Status was all important to Hamid's mom and she felt she had found an ideal prospective bride for her beloved son. Pretty, sophisticated and rich—perfect daughter-in-law material!

But Hamid had not signed up to his mother's plans. We were seeing each other more and more often, and it became evident that he wanted to be with me as much as I wanted to be with him. The first flurry of emotions was gradually shifting into deeper feelings, the bond between us growing stronger by the day.

Much to his mom's disappointment, Hamid broke up with his girlfriend, justifying his decision by saying that he did not want to mislead a girl he did not really love. Fun-loving Hamid found the prospective bride selected by his mother very uptight. Determined to marry as soon as possible, she adopted a conservative, grown-up behavior that suited the role, but Hamid found her boring. I was far more outgoing and playful, even if shy by nature, and Hamid loved that about me.

By then, we had started dating, but kept our romance secret even from his sister. Hamid did not share that information with his mom either, knowing she did not approve of me and my family. Parvin would no doubt blame me for his decision not to marry Miss Perfect. So, he kept silent.

· · ·

Hamid was my first boyfriend and my first love. Puberty brought in a growing interest in boys, but I had not acted upon it so far. A couple of years earlier, I had a teenage crush on a blue-eyed boy called Kia who lived near my middle school. He did not even know I existed. Half the students in my school were smitten with Kia, who basked in his popularity. He was a total player, carefully timing his arrivals and departures from home to coincide with the exact time our school let out. As he rode his bad-ass red motorcycle, he knew all the girls were watching. He relished his star status among young female students. His phone number was floating around the school, passed on from girl to girl. He probably got dozens of calls a day from our school mates.

Two girls I knew were regularly hanging out with him. Both of them called Sara, they were gorgeous and from wealthy progressive families who spent their summer vacations in Europe. No way I could compete with them! Regardless, I plucked up the courage to call Kia's house a few times, covering the mouthpiece and just listening to his voice without saying a word. Other infatuated students, impressed with Kia's smooth performance, were doing the same even if they, too, knew they were no match for the cool Saras.

Apart from glamorous bad boy Kia, no man had attracted my attention so far. Unlike Kia, Hamid was not an unattainable target. Our relationship was grounded in reality and involved genuine feelings. Hamid gave me my first taste of grown-up love. When we started dating, I floated on cloud nine, pinching myself that this popular guy with an oversized personality had chosen me!

Hamid had a face that was both ugly and beautiful in equal parts, with full lips, a big, crooked Middle eastern nose, and intense, brooding eyes. His tall, athletic build reminded me of a boxer—wound up tight like a spring and ready for a fight. But he was not a boxer, he was a water polo player and had the broad shoulders of strong swimmers. He moved with the effortless grace and confidence of a sportsman who trusts his body.

At 17, I had never been in love, I had never been loved the way he loved me, and touched with the tenderness and the affection he showed me. My feelings for Hamid were deep and strong, and they colored my entire life. His charming and confident personality acted like a magnet and I loved that he frequently expressed his desire to be with me. His willingness to take risks so we could have together made him attractive in my eyes, irresistible even.

Those early days of my relationship with Hamid were nothing short of magical. I never felt more cherished than when we both crept around the city looking for hidden spots where we could spend time alone. Hamid was my first love and his passionate embraces evoked heady feelings and intoxicating new sensations.

With his friends and water polo teammates, my boyfriend was loud and outgoing, always joking and appearing supremely self-confident—at times overly so. With me, he showed his more sensitive, vulnerable side. Underneath the jock was a fragile personality, easily affected by the blows of everyday life.

We spent hours talking about our dreams, our future, and complained bitterly—and at times unfairly—about our parents and the obstacles they set in our way. We were kids, enamored with each other, and with love itself.

.   .   .

With our families against us, the first couple of years of our romance felt like the Tehran version of the Montagues and Capulets. We were very aware of the obstacles in our way. Hamid's mother was a snob and she had her heart set on her son marrying into a wealthy family. I was not a suitable girlfriend in her eyes.

On my side of the equation, I knew my father would oppose our relationship: Dating was not a concept he could grasp. Dad stemmed from a patriarchal background and would never allow a man to come near me before we were legally wed or at least engaged to be married.

Far from deterring us, the forbidden nature of our romance, combined with the repressive circumstances we all faced in Iran, acted as powerful, addictive drug. I was still in high school, but I displayed the passion of a grown woman determined to be with the man she loved. Neither the risk of facing punishment at the hands of my father or disappointing my mother could quell my obsession. I felt safe with Hamid. High on love, I was prepared to take unimaginable risks to spend time with him.

•   •   •

Tradition demanded that if a man was interested in a girl, he had to make his intentions clear by turning up at her parents' house, with his own family, and asking for permission to marry her. My dad remained firmly attached to these customs, which followed a specific ritual. He had married Mom without even catching a glimpse of her before the wedding and would not understand the love Hamid and I felt for each other. To him, marriage came first, then love developed.

Once the prospective groom and his family were seated, the blushing would-be bride entered the room with a tray of freshly brewed black tea, pouring it for each of the assembled guests into small crystal teacups reserved for special occasions. The tea had to be brewed just right, to achieve a rich dark reddish color, as evidence of her domestic skills.

When my sister Niloo got engaged, she had to go through this ceremonial. Her Iranian husband was studying in the US and he agreed to meet prospective brides recommended by his parents during a visit back to Iran. My parents and his knew each other and arranged for their children to meet. Niloo and the young man hit it off. My mom encouraged the match, confident in the belief that her eldest daughter would have a better life in the US. Niloo was the first member of our family who left Iran after the revolution. My mom's assessment of the marriage proved correct: My sister and her husband went on to have two children and they remain married to this day.

I love tea and could fool a potential groom with a good brew, but that was the extent of my home skills. In Iran, tea is associated with a daily custom that I love: After waking up refreshed from our afternoon nap, we sat down, like most Persian families, for a cup of tea accompanied by delicious Iranian pastries, heavily influenced by the French and the British.

Teatime satisfied my sweet tooth—I did not associate it with a display of wifely credentials. In fact, I did not know the first thing about cooking. To me, the entire ritual assessing the girl's talents was silly. I could not understand the purpose or logic behind a ceremony that reduced a young woman to a domestic servant. Nor did I ever want my parents to negotiate a marriage on my behalf. It felt demeaning that my fate—any woman's fate—should be determined through a transaction, an agreement hotly negotiated by third parties who discussed terms and conditions.

Gold was the main currency in marriage negotiations and the two families discussed how much gold the groom was prepared to pay for the bride. If a husband left his wife, for instance, he would have to pay her family the agreed amount in gold coins. In modern practice, gold coins rarely changed hands and the discussions were a formality, but I rebelled against the transactional nature of the agreement and a custom that ascribed a monetary value to a woman.

By the time Hamid and I started dating, many progressive Iranians had abandoned these traditions and young couples married of their own free will in greater numbers. My father, however, did not subscribe to the notion of a love marriage. He was not ready to modernize and abandon old-fashioned ways.

•   •   •

Marriage could not be further from our mind. Hamid and I felt far too young to settle down. I had not even graduated high school and he was attending college. We wanted to have fun and were happy just to explore and enjoy our budding relationship. I started playing hooky from school to spend more time with my beloved. Transported to a fairy tale, I could not keep away from Hamid for more than a few hours.

When the phone rang in our apartment, I raced from my bedroom to reach it first.

"Who is it?" Mom shouted from the kitchen.

"It's just Aram," I lied, my heart aflutter at the sound of my boyfriend's voice. "We have to discuss a school assignment."

Hamid and I spent hours chatting about all and nothing and expressing our love for each other. When one of our parents picked up the phone, we hung up without a word, praying that we had not awoken their suspicion.

Part of the thrill was coming up with creative ways to see each other. Both our homes were off-limits most of the time and we could not hang out in the streets or in cafes without facing harassment or arrest by the morality police.

Since we lived on opposite sides of the same street, we coordinated our schedules and timed our morning departure from home. Ready for school, I kept watch from my window and rushed out when I saw Hamid leave his tower block.

On the pavement, we barely acknowledged each other, but blood rushed to my face when we brushed against each other, our fingers meeting for a few second. I kept my fist tightly closed around the note Hamid slipped into my hand, rushing to the school bathroom to read it away from prying eyes.

"You are the light of my life, baby! I love you," the note stated in Hamid's messy scrawl. "5 PM in the courtyard."

For a while, the grimy elevator room at the top of their high-rise building became a love nest. We did not care that the cubbyhole was dusty and filled with dirty elevator parts. In each other's arms for hours on end, love made us blind to our grubby surroundings. Eventually, we were chased away from our shelter by a maintenance man who stumbled onto us while looking for his tools.

"What are you doing here!", The man thundered. What we were doing here was obvious. "Don't come back or I'll tell your parents."

We apologized and left, guffawing as soon as we were out of sight. No matter! We were in love—no one and nothing could stand in our way.

"You're in a good mood," Mom said as I sauntered into the house, giddy with excitement after a brief encounter with Hamid on my way back from school.

"Yes, I had a good day at school," I replied. "I did better than expected in the math test."

Mom must have been suspicious, but she did not probe further. Dad could not blame her for allowing a relationship she was unaware of.

As our romance progressed, we got more daring. During my parents' long trips to the US, I snuck Hamid into our home while Roya was at work. He did the same when his mom and sister went out. I would rush over to his home and hang out with him for as long as was safe.

If I craned my neck, from my first-floor bedroom window, I could catch a corner of Hamid's balcony on the 15th floor of the tower block opposite. We devised a flag system with red scarves to take advantage of the rare moments when we had our homes to ourselves. Whenever I caught a glimpse of crimson in the corner of my window, my heart went wild and I pretended to go out and meet a friend. In the elevator taking me to my beloved's apartment, I felt dizzy with love and lust.

After we lost access to the maintenance room, we looked for new secret hideouts. Some days, we would just drive aimlessly around Tehran for hours, Hamid at the wheel and me sitting next to him in the passenger seat holding his hand. This was not without risk. We could get stopped and have our identities checked. We knew that relationships outside wedlock were strictly prohibited, but we hardly considered what was at stake. We were in seventh heaven, and when Hamid looked into my eyes, I felt like the most beautiful woman in the world. "Is this what love feels like?" I wondered. I was prepared to risk anything to be with my boyfriend. He was my first love and, innocent as I was, I thought it would be the last.

·　　·　　·

Surprisingly, we managed to keep our relationship a secret beyond our tight-knit group of friends for a long time. Several of my school friends were also dating. They, too, were bypassing official restrictions and this brought us closer together. We attended parties and even traveled outside the cities as a group on a few occasions without attracting scrutiny.

I rarely had to tell outright lies to my parents. Most of the time, I was just economical with the truth. "I am spending the evening with Mona", I would say, omitting to mention that she had a boyfriend and we would all attend a mixed-gender party. My parents would have had a fit!

My sister Roya, my loyal confidante, knew that I was seeing Hamid and she covered for us on several occasions. Already in her twenties, she had a successful job and faced far fewer constraints on the home front than I did. Our parents accepted that she was an independent woman, partly because her salary contributed to the family income after my dad's business collapsed due to war damage.

Roya moved in foreign and diplomatic circles, and she invited Hamid and I to join her on several occasions when she attended parties held by her friends. The three of us also ventured out on road trips outside Tehran. She never breathed a word to our parents.

Drunk with love, I thought of Hamid day and night. I spent more and more time with my darling, and schoolwork suffered. As my class attendance dropped, so did my grades. Hamid, who had been studying engineering, dropped out of college entirely. It was not an option open to me and I envied him for walking away from studies he did not enjoy. His decision to quit would haunt us both later, however.

Unaware of the underlying reason for my poor school performance, my parents scolded me for not studying hard and spending too much time with friends. I was never academically inclined, but until then, I had achieved decent grades, even if no subject beyond art and English interested me. But I was no longer a diligent student! I was a young woman madly in love.

My parents' disapproval peaked when I failed the finals in year 3 and was held back. High school in Iran was tough and the exams very competitive— somewhat the equivalent of early college years in the States. No slacking was possible if you wanted to succeed. Paying a price for spending too much time with my boyfriend, I had to re-do the year and sit the exams once more. Dad threatened to ground me. My parents' wrath and disappointment hurt, but not as much as the prospect of not being allowed to see Hamid!

•　　•　　•

Looking back at this period of my youth, I see that the early days of my relationship with Hamid were the happiest of my time in Iran. The fear of being found out and the obstacles that stood in the way of our budding love only magnified our feelings for each other. Hamid was considerate and romantic—the perfect boyfriend! I believed, and still do to this day in spite of what happened later, that he truly loved me during this heady period. Roya had plenty of opportunities to observe us together and she watched carefully how he interacted with me. She was fond of him. "He's a good guy", she said, impressed with his politeness and respectful attitude .

By the time the war ended, living conditions in Tehran felt a bit easier, even if the economy was in poor shape. The restrictions on our private lives persisted but the level of enforcement ebbed and flowed with the rhythm of local politics. During more relaxed periods, usually brief, my friends and I could loosen our headscarves and let a few strands of hair show. Then, the lid would slam shut and stricter control was enforced again.

Unmarried boys and girls were still banned from mixing. But we gathered at our friend's house with more open-minded parents. I still had to contend with my dad's archaic attitude but I became skilled at averting his suspicion, and for a long time managed to go undetected.

"Do you want me to pick you up?" Dad asked whenever I went out, allegedly to meet my friends from school.

"No need, Dad, Aram's mom will drop me off."

After a party that involved boys—and Hamid—I always arranged to be dropped off. I only called on Dad's services as a driver when I saw my close female friends. Needless to say, having a wild party with girls and boys drinking and dancing to music at our house was out of the question. My father sometimes consumed alcohol, although he was not a heavy drinker, but us kids were not allowed to drink. At most, I could invite a handful of girlfriends for tea and cake on my birthday. The only boys who could show up at our house were relatives.

. . .

Avoiding the Morality Police when we were in public venues, attending parties or driving around Tehran or outside the city required careful planning. Thankfully, our small group of friends included several siblings. Before I dated Hamid, his sister Pooneh had been a close friend who often attended the same parties as we did. On more than one occasion, having her as a fellow passenger in the car proved useful: Pooneh did not know that her brother and I were dating. If we were stopped, she could claim that I was in the car as her friend, and her brother was driving us both to a family event. It did mean, however, that Hamid and I had to be careful in her presence and avoid getting too close. We knew she would report to their mother.

If the Morality Police, alerted by the noise or duplicitous neighbors, turned up at a house where a party was held, complicit parents who understood that young people needed to let off steam would apologize, promise to turn down the music and claim their children were being unruly with visiting cousins.

Although alcohol was involved, our parties were quite tame, at least by Western standards. Two or three of the guys played the guitar and I remember us all belting out Iranian songs, recorded by famous Iranian singers in exile, whose music was smuggled into the country.

The guitar was also an essential travel accessory when we ventured out of town for a few days. Most of my friends were from well-to-do families that had secondary residences on the Caspian Sea coast or in ski resorts. These villas were a perfect hideaway for us young people. Outside the capital, militias were often less vigilant. Still, we had to be careful not to be stopped on the road. On one or two occasions, the boys managed to bribe our way out of trouble after we were intercepted.

On public beaches along the Caspian Sea, bathers were segregated by sex. Even when swimming, we had to keep our modesty. Bikinis were banned! Our friend's villa, fortunately, was in a luxury complex that had a private beach where we could all congregate with less risk of being overlooked.

With my tender lover by my side, surrounded by friends I had known for years, I felt perfectly content. With hindsight, I marvel that we even succeeded in carving out these slices of happiness in difficult circumstances. We were bursting with optimism. Animated by the irrepressible spirit of youth, we were determined to push the tight boundaries that constrained us, no matter the costs.

But clouds were already gathering that would soon threaten our idyll.

• • •

Hamid and I had been secretly dating for a couple of years when his mom and his sister got wind of our romance. Since Hamid had broken up with his previous girlfriend, he had shown no obvious inclination to find a replacement. His mom invited a succession of wealthy girls to their house, hoping to arouse his interest, to no avail. Something was up!

Nosy neighbors or family friends soon confirmed her suspicions after spotting us around town. Before we knew it, our secret was out and everything changed.

Hamid's mother went nuclear. How could her precious son choose a girl from a middle-class, unassuming family? He was lowering the family standards. She wanted wealth, prestige, influence!

Parvin started issuing threats, warning me to stay away from him "or else." On several occasions, she cornered me when she saw me on the street, since we were neighbors. But mostly, she drafted her daughter to do her dirty work. Pooneh would call me at home, lecture me and relay her mom's ultimatums. Aware that my dad would be horrified and furious to learn that I had a steady boyfriend, Parvin tried to blackmail me. "If you don't stop seeing Hamid, I'll tell your father." She knew there would be hell to pay!

She worked on her son, too, crying, begging and bullying him. When her campaign was unsuccessful, she drafted in Pooneh to influence Hamid. The more the pressure from his mom and sister intensified, the closer Hamid and I felt to each other. Our bond was getting stronger: It was us against the world and nothing was going to stop us.

Or so I thought. Many months later, I would discover that Parvin's drip-drip of poisonous allegations against me was slowly entering Hamid's consciousness. At the time, though, he was standing firm, by my side.

Eventually, Parvin's frustration boiled over and she pulled the trigger: She told my dad! I will never forget that wretched day. I was at a friend's house when Dad arrived to pick me up, as planned. But as soon as I got into the car, I knew something was wrong. His face was like thunder and fury was oozing out of his stocky body.

After driving in silence for a few minutes, he let go of the steering wheel and, without warning, slapped me hard across the face with a ferocious backhand. Such was his power that my ears were ringing. I knew right away that Hamid's mother had done her dirty work.

Dad launched into an angry diatribe, pouring out anger, disappointment and disgust. "You are a complete disgrace," he shouted. "You have shamed me. You have shamed our family."

Unable to stop, he vented all the way home. How could I act so brazenly with a neighborhood boy, embarrassing the family and damaging its reputation?

"What will people say?" He yelled.

When we got home, his wrath boiled over and things got worse. He dragged me to my room, slapped me a few more times before roughly pushing me into the room and slamming the door. Curled up on the floor, head bowed, I could hear him ranting loudly through the closed door.

In his eyes, dating or even spending time alone with a man who is not your husband—or at least your fiancé—was completely unacceptable. At least, this was not behavior he would tolerate from his daughters.

Before he left Iran, my brother Joseph had dated a girl for a while. He brought his girlfriend to our house several times and openly attended parties with her at friends' houses. Even when Joseph stayed out all night, my father never said a word. The rules were different for boys and girls.

The double standards made my blood boil. I was outraged! I knew that some of my girlfriends had far more adventurous love lives than mine. Compared to them, I was one of the good girls. I had not dated anyone before Hamid, and I was 17 when our relationship began. It took nearly two years before I even let him touch me.

None of this mattered to my dad. Even his nieces were free to do as they pleased. But for his youngest daughter, he set the bar much higher!

CHAPTER FIVE

A BAD DECISION

"The rose and the thorn, and sorrow and gladness are linked together.
–Saadi

Our secret was out! Hamid and I were no longer alone in our loved-up bubble. His mother and my parents were now interested parties. Our fate was no longer entirely in our own hands.

I did not notice it straight away, but around that time, Hamid's behavior started to shift. After his dad passed away, the burden of taking care of his mom and sister had passed onto his shoulders. This responsibility was thrust upon his shoulders when in fact he was still a lost kid.

The family had been well off, but money became tighter once the father was no longer there to secure an income. Hamid's mom Parvin had never worked— holding a job was not the norm for women of her generation. Far from being humbled by her bereavement and new financial circumstances, she clung on to delusions of grandeur that alienated those around them and did nothing to help the family.

During the heady days of our early romance, Hamid and I occasionally quarreled. He was at times jealous and possessive and grew irritated when he thought I looked at other men. Once, when we attended a friend's wedding, he accused me of staring at another guest for too long.

"Stop looking at him!" he hissed in the middle of the evening.

I was stunned, because I was not at all interested in the man in question. Hamid's jealous imagination was in overdrive. Several similar incidents occurred over the months. Naive as I was in those days, I found Hamid's paranoia mildly flattering, seeing it as proof of his strong feelings for me. I thought it showed how much he loved me!

Time would teach me the hard way that control and possessiveness are about exercising power. They are not demonstrations of love. Hamid's attempts to rule over me and police my behavior were warning signs, but I failed to notice them.

His dad has been dead for a while by then, and my boyfriend was showing signs of buckling under the weight of family expectations. How could this college dropout provide for the household when he had no skills? Hamid was a man-child, unwilling to step up to his responsibilities. His mom had always held him on a pedestal, indulging his every whim. Without the firm hand of his father to guide him, the spoiled brat in him took over. He wanted everything fast and easy.

After abandoning education, he also quit his water polo team. With no structure left to impose any discipline to his life, he started smoking and drinking in ever larger quantities. He even encouraged me to join him, introducing me to alcohol and cigarettes. At one point, he persuaded me to try marijuana, but I hallucinated so badly that I pledged never to touch the stuff again.

Reality was infringing upon our fairy tale. Hamid was no longer my sunny, carefree lover—the boy who battled the world with me. He was becoming a troubled young man, a Peter Pan refusing to grow up. Over the months, his behavior grew more volatile, but I never questioned the relationship. I loved him and stood by him, attributing his volatile reactions to the pressure of being in charge and his mother's disapproval of me.

Parvin also noticed the changes and she had a culprit in mind: Me. Her perfect son was incapable of wrongdoing in her eyes: I was to blame. Only a person below their social standing could drive Hamid to smoke and drink! She also believed I was the reason he quit college, of course.

In reality, Hamid's decision to end his education was his, and his alone. He had not consulted me, and I only learned about that he had quit school after he stopped attending class for a month or so. For my part, after failing my exams and re-doing a year in high school, I redoubled my efforts to improve my score. My hurt pride—I was competitive and could not accept failure—rather than my parents' constant lecturing caused me to focus more on schoolwork. As we headed toward graduation, I spent long nights at my friend Aram's house, studying with her until the small hours of the morning.

Decades later, as we reminisced about our school days, she thanked me. "If it had not been for you, I would never have graduated," she told me. My determination to succeed and the hours we spent studying enabled her to graduate with flying colors.

Hamid's mom Parvin knew none of this. Nor would she have acknowledged my achievements even if she had. She appeared to keep a tally of my failings and the offenses I had allegedly committed against her family and her precious son. As it expanded, so did Parvin's hate and animosity towards me.

While her handsome and successful husband was alive, Parvin focused all her attention on him. He was a jovial man with a curled-up mustache groomed to perfection who commanded respect and affection. After he died, Parvin's social universe fell apart. She had lost her compass and her place in society.

Hamid was the only male member of the family—all she had left. The way she saw it, I was taking him away from her, depriving their family of the financial support that a wealthy father-in-law would provide and bringing nothing in exchange. She believed that I was to blame for turning Hamid into a person she could no longer recognize.

The one constant in her life was her sense of superiority. Even as the family circumstances changed, finances grew tight and her social standing plummeted, Parvin never abandoned the notion that her family was far superior to mine. Money and prestige were the only currencies she recognized, and my middle-class parents did not make the cut. We were not poor, in fact we were comfortable thanks to Dad's hard work, but we did not belong to the wealthy elite that was her yardstick.

Whatever her reasons, she took against me with a vengeance. Looking back from a distance of over two decades, I wonder if she was aware of her son's weaknesses. Maybe she realized, deep down, that Hamid could not be successful on his own. He needed a rich wife—and a powerful father-in-law who would give him a management position or support him as he set up his own business. Her son not only lacked skills but also the drive, acumen and determination it takes to build a successful business, or even rise through the ranks as an employee in a good company, like my sister Roya. But Parvin found it far easier to assign blame than to reflect on the way she had brought him up.

Treating her son like a prince, perfect in every way, and never holding him accountable for his actions was not the best approach to parenting. All she achieved was to turn him into an entitled, work-shy man expecting instant success.

But questioning her own actions was not part of Parvin's mental toolbox. Finger pointing was!

·   ·   ·

Working less and less, Hamid was drinking more and more, creating tension in our relationship. Still, I found excuses for his behavior and remained blind to his shortcomings. My dad was less forgiving. In a desperate attempt to make me see sense after he found out that I was still seeing Hamid, he sold our apartment and moved our family to another neighborhood uptown, further away from my boyfriend's condo.

Tehran sits on a slope at the foothills of the Alborz Mountains. The closer you get to the mountain range that dominates the city, the fancier the neighborhood. Our first family home was in the lower reaches of the city, then we moved to Park-e Saie, near a large avenue called Vali-e Asr, still referred to by many as Pahlavi, after the Shah.

This time, my dad moved us further uptown to Ghandi neighborhood, a part of Tehran that houses many foreign embassies and consulates. He thought that putting some physical distance between us would make it harder for me to see Hamid, and our young love would wither and die.

He was also concerned that our neighbors knew that I was dating, and he felt profoundly embarrassed. Reputation was everything for a man like my dad. In his old-fashioned mind, my behavior reflected on him, our family and the neighborly community we lived in. I had let everyone down.

Our move meant that Hamid and I had to cover longer distances to see each other. We could no longer wave from our respective windows. On the positive side, we were less likely to run into Parvin who could no longer accost me in the street to issue threats. We just had to be even more discreet and creative to find opportunities to be together.

Dad's radar was now on full alert and we were not successful for long. He may not have achieved a high education level, but my father was sharp, experienced and streetwise. I had inherited some of his street smarts, so for a few months, we competed in a daily cat-and-mouse game. Dad saw through whatever tricks Hamid and I came up with. Power was on his side, too. His next step was not to punish or lecture me. Instead, he confronted Hamid on the street one morning, after waiting by his apartment building.

Shaped by a rough life and upbringing that had made him tough as nails, my dad could be scary if he wanted to. Tattoos covered his arms, chest and back, acquired in the 1950s when he was in his twenties. At the time, tattoos were not the hip form of expression they are today. They signaled strength and power and were meant to intimidate. And intimidating my dad was!

He gave Hamid one last warning.

"Leave my daughter alone or there will be consequences, young man!"

Dad did not spell out what the repercussions might be, but Hamid knew he was not joking. However, my lover was not about to walk away, in spite of his legitimate concerns. "I love your daughter and would like to marry her, Sir!" Hamid said.

Getting married was the only way Hamid and I could continue to see each other. But Dad remained opposed. At first, he said no and tried to convince Hamid that it was a bad idea: my prospective husband was too young and in no position to support a wife, let alone a family. My father was also acutely aware of Parvin's contempt for our family, which was offensive.

"You have to talk to your mother first," Dad said.

In a rare show of strength, Hamid snapped back and told Dad he would not stay away from me, no matter what.

"Mr. Meknat, Sir" he said, "I love and respect your daughter. I don't have any bad intentions; I truly care for her. Allow us to get married. I know my mom will come around eventually. I am her only son, you see, she doesn't have any other choice."

That afternoon, my dad sat me down, my mom sitting beside him. Underneath his tough shell, there was a soft heart. He could not stand seeing his youngest daughter lock herself in her room and cry her eyes out all day. My parents had sensible advice for me, even if I was too loved up at the time to appreciate it. I should either break up with Hamid—though by then, they had little hope this would happen—or at least insist that he should get his mother on board first.

In my eyes, Parvin was only Hamid's mom, an obstacle to our happiness that could be overcome. With more experience of Iran's social structure and class divides, my parents saw her in a different light: They identified her type—a snob who would always look down upon the likes of them. She spelled trouble, they thought.

My parents understood that Parvin would go ballistic when she eventually found out that Hamid and I had gone behind her back and got married. Having experienced brutal treatment at the hands of Dad's relatives, my mom knew first-hand that a domineering mother-in-law could make life very difficult for a young bride. My parents' forecasts turned out to be accurate, but I brushed them aside.

I also rejected their generous offer to send me to America to continue my education or do whatever I wanted. The more they tried to bribe me or put pressure on me, the more I stood my ground. Hamid and I would be together! End of story.

I finally wore them out. Since we were not going to stop seeing each other, we should be legally married. At least, we would not get into trouble with the Morality Police and the family honor would be restored. My parents wanted to shut down the nosy gossipers who had been whispering about my seeing Hamid. I personally did not care, but my parents valued their opinion.

With hindsight, I realize that my parents tried their best to protect me. Iranian society was still conservative.

Before the revolution, the educated elite had become more westernized, but a significant portion of the population abided by more patriarchal values, which were later forcibly imposed on the entire population, on religious ground, by the revolutionary regime. Societies where gender imbalances are so stark, women always end up carrying the blame when tension flares up in families. My parents did not want me to be caught up in the crossfire.

. . .

My engagement party was bittersweet because it was combined with a farewell party for my sister Roya, who was leaving Iran to join my other siblings in the US. The steady trickle of family members leaving Iran was continuing. Niloo, Joseph, now my beloved Roya—my big sister, my rock, my confidante... Here I was, simultaneously celebrating my engagement to the man I loved and saying goodbye to the one person who had supported me unconditionally. I should have felt on top of the world: After a drawn-out campaign of attrition, I had won a major victory and would marry the man I loved!

But my feelings were mixed. We invited friends and family for the occasion, but only my side of the family. Hamid was not yet prepared to talk to his mother. Another red flag in our relationship I failed to notice!

The engagement party took place in our apartment. I should remember every detail of this momentous occasion, but I was too conflicted to store the memories.

My parents set aside their misgivings for the day and did their best to make it a festive event.

I dressed up in a long, pink hand-me-down dress sent from California by one of my very stylish cousins. It looked amazing on her but it was two sizes too big for my skinny figure. With my hair done up, crowned by an ugly tiara and so much make up that I barely recognized myself, I was decked out like a dowdy village bride. But I was only a 19-year-old girl. Self-conscious about my mouth full of metal braces, I could not even look at the camera and smile. Instead, photos of the day show me looking down at the small diamond engagement ring Hamid had bought me a couple of months earlier.

Roya left shortly after that night, leaving a huge void in my life. I tried to focus on my upcoming marriage and spent as much time as possible with my soon-to-be-husband to distract me from her absence.

•   •   •

A few days before Hamid and me legally married, my mother came into my room to tell me that she had made an appointment with a female gynecologist, who would examine me and provide a certificate stating that I was still intact. Virginity was a highly prized asset in Iran and my mom, like most of her peers, worried about other people's opinion. We needed proof that I was a virgin, in case Hamid's mother ever claimed that I had come into her family "tainted."

"Knowing her, we should be prepared for anything," Mom said.

What in the world was my mother talking about? We were not in the 1800s! But my parents held firmly onto their conservative views. There was no arguing with them about their outdated way of thinking.

I looked down, staring intently at the red flowers on the vibrant Persian rug covering my bedroom floor. How could I tell her? I knew my parents' view on pre-marital sex, and I was terrified of their reaction. Ashamed, too, because I would drop in their esteem.

I thought of the day I had lost my virginity, nearly two years into our relationship. Hamid had his parents' apartment to himself that day. His mom and sister had gone out, and we knew that they wouldn't be back for hours. We were ready to take our love and relationship to the next level. I was afraid, timid and unsure, but I loved him and wanted to prove my devotion to him. In my young mind, taking that irreversible step would demonstrate that he was the one and only for me and I wanted to be with him forever.

I braced myself, "Mom.... I am not a virgin anymore." I said, my voice shaking.

Her eyes nearly popped out of her head as she looked at me, horrified and disgusted. She went hysterical. "How could you do this to me? You are a disgrace," she screamed. Yup, I was a disgrace. I had heard that one before.

As Mom slammed the door on her way out, all I could think was, "I've failed her again". I was ashamed of myself for disobeying my parents and acting in a way they considered immoral. I did not share their views and beliefs, and I had only slept with one man, the man I loved and was about to marry, but the shame still burned deep inside me.

Their conservative views had been drilled into me since infancy and I could not shake them off easily. I desperately wanted my parents' approval, especially my mother's. Now that Roya had left, I needed her on my side more than ever. I wanted Mom to understand and approve of my choices. But she made it clear I had failed her. She knew Dad would get very angry and kept that secret to herself to spare me dire consequences.__

I will never forget the somber look on my dad's face the day we went to the courthouse to sign the marriage register. To this day, it is one of the biggest regrets of my life. It pained me to see this big, strong and proud man, well respected in the community, looking utterly defeated—and I was the cause of his distress. I am sure he harbored dreams of a better future for his little girl and hated to see me get married in semi-secrecy at a courthouse, in the absence of the groom's family, which didn't approve of the match. I, too, had hoped to marry in grander circumstances if I was ever going to get married. Marriage, wedding, none of that was something I dreamed about or prioritized as a young girl, but some of my friends had held big wedding celebrations and if I was going to get married, I wanted to make it memorable as well. But we signed the piece of paper and I went home a married woman.

I should have put my foot down and refused to go through with the ceremony until Hamid had told his family that we were getting married. But I wanted to avoid causing tension in our relationship. I chose to believe him when he said that his mother would eventually come around.

As a result, we had a low-key wedding with no celebration and no white dress. More importantly, our two families did not come together to joyfully mark the union of their children. Our marriage was just a legal formality to appease my dad and the authorities. We signed the papers at the courthouse and went home.

While we waited in the courthouse for our turn to appear in front of the marriage officer, my dad turned to me and said: " If you go through with this, don't ever think of coming back." Did he hope that this last-minute threat would cause me to abandon my plans and call the whole thing off? Probably not. But I took his warning very seriously: I was crossing a threshold and there would be no return.

Divorce was not an option in my father's eyes. His youngest sister had been married three times, divorced twice, and was on her way to the third divorce. She was the one who had kicked my mother in her stomach while she was pregnant with my brother Joseph. After her marriages broke down, she was largely shunned by the family, which saw her as a troublemaker who broke even more rules than I did. In the eyes of the family, she was a "disgrace" and Dad did not want me to be perceived this way.

After Hamid and I put our signatures on the dotted line and legally became husband and wife, we all went back to my parents' apartment. On the ride home, we were all subdued. My dad was in the driving seat, my mom by his side while Hamid and I held hands in the back seat. "My husband," I thought. "Nothing can get between us now." But even that thought did not lift my spirits. We should have been happy and celebrating our big day. Instead, we all sat in uncomfortable silence.

When we got home, my mom prepared a delicious chicken and eggplant stew with fragrant saffron rice—a traditional festive dish chosen because it was one of my favorites. The festive treat was meant to emphasize that today was a momentous occasion, but I felt empty. My wedding day was nothing like I had imagined. It was a weird occasion and I felt Roya's absence acutely.

•   •   •

Because Hamid's mom was still unaware that we had married, my husband and I could not live together. For a couple of years, I lived at home with my parents while Hamid continued to live with his mom and sister.

We settled into a new routine, seeing each other every day. He often slept at my place. I found a job as a receptionist in a medical practice run by a husband and wife. He was an orthopedist and his wife a dermatologist. The job did not excite me, but it kept me busy and provided a small income.

The main change was that Hamid and I no longer had to sneak around and hide from my parents or the authorities. We could go out, have dinner in public and walk in the park holding hands without fear of being imprisoned or fined. But our freedom was still limited by Hamid's insistence that his family must not find out. We avoided places where we risked running into his mother or sister and stayed away from people likely to snitch. It felt strange because we did not live on the opposite side of the city. We frequented the same places and knew many people in common. The whole situation weighed on me.

Still, being married made it easier to go on ski trips or travel up north to the Caspian Sea beaches with loyal friends. I no longer had to lie to my parents and pretend I was going out with my girlfriends. Not stressing about Dad was a major improvement.

For a couple of months, Hamid and I had my parents' house to ourselves. He could have lived with me full-time during this period, but he insisted on keeping up the pretense that he was single and returned to his mom's home frequently. My parents had gone to the US to visit Niloo, Joseph and now Roya, who had all settled in the same Southern California area. I was their only child left in Iran!

The secrecy surrounding our marriage was beginning to irritate me. I did not want to be a secret! Plus, I knew that, as long as Parvin did not know that her son was married, she would try to set him up the daughters of wealthy family friends if she got a chance. I had witnessed the way she pushed women right into his lap.

My frustration was growing, triggering rows with Hamid. But I had to bide my time and keep my unhappiness from my parents after they returned. Having shattered their expectations with my low-key registry office marriage, I did not want to upset them any further.

So, I stayed silent and secretly hoped that my husband's mom or sister would somehow find out about our marriage. A storm was brewing. It took a while to build up, but it was just a matter of time until it broke out.

CHAPTER SIX

FALSE START

"Don't grieve. Anything you lose comes round in another form."
–Rumi

When Roya announced that she got engaged to an American man, a short couple of years after arriving in the US, I was not surprised. My sister was a strong and independent woman and I always trusted that she would quickly find her feet in her new homeland and build a life for herself. She knew what she wanted and went after it fiercely. She was used to international life: Her friends back in Tehran were mostly educated upper-class professionals and diplomats from Europe and South American countries.

My strong sister was now in her element. She had never wanted to settle for a meaningless life as the trophy wife of an overbearing Iranian husband in Tehran, surrounded by a few children. Roya would not accept the small existence led by many young women we knew in Iran. She had courage, intelligence and ambition, and was determined to forge her own path.

Before she left, I often begged her to take me to the parties she attended most weekends. As a teenager, I found Westerners with blonde hair and blue eyes the most exotic and attractive creatures—maybe because, in my mind, their relaxed behavior epitomized the freedom and wealth that was not available to us. She complied on several occasions and allowed me to take Hamid with me. I envied her lifestyle and her fearlessness, but really, I just admired her.

My dad, as strict as he was, never gave Roya a hard time or attempted to curtail her independence the way he disciplined me. My sister commanded respect from all around her, our parents included. Her approach was maybe less confrontational than mine—she naturally knew how to get her way without alienating our parents.

After long hours at the office, she was often exhausted by the end of the day, but if she wanted to attend a party and come home after midnight, she did just that. My parents trusted her more than any of their other kids. After an Iraqi bomb destroyed the business my father had invested in and our family lost most of its assets, Roya helped my parents financially. This put her in a position of power. Even if Mom and Dad were tempted to boss her around, they could not. She was a girl boss before youth entrepreneurship became a thing. I was delighted that Roya had found love in California, but I missed her in my daily life in Tehran.

. . .

A few months after the exciting announcement, my parents started to make plans to attend her wedding in California. Traveling to the US was complicated as there was no longer a US embassy or consulate in our country after the Iranian revolution and the hostage crisis. Iranians had to go to Turkey, Dubai or other parts of the world to apply for a visa to visit the United States.

Shortly after the Shah was toppled in 1979 and the religious government took over, revolutionary students stormed the American embassy and took 52 members of personnel and civilians hostage. America was considered the Great Satan, and a popular slogan, repeated ad nauseam during demonstrations, marches and after the weekly Friday mass prayer, was "Marg Bar Amrika" (Death to America). The strength of anti-western sentiment behind this slogan struck me as odd because most of the people around me, my parents, members of my extended family, but also my friends' relatives, dream of leaving Iran and living in the West. Hostage crisis at the US embassy lasted 444 days. In retaliation, the US seized the Iranian Embassy in Washington DC. After protracted negotiations and a failed rescue attempt that cost President Jimmy Carter a second term in office, the American hostages were eventually released in January 1981. But their kidnap, an unprecedented breach of diplomatic protocol, severed the links between Iran and the US and continues to cast a long shadow on their relations today.

The main consequence for us, ordinary Iranians, was that traveling abroad, particularly to the US, became a lot harder and required carefully and costly planning, months ahead.

. . .

I missed Roya terribly and decided I would accompany my parents to Turkey and try my luck with a US visa. Nothing would make me happier than to attend my sister's wedding, which promised to be a big Iranian American celebration. All my siblings and cousins who had left Iran would attend. I did not want to be left out. Our family had been separated for too long!

For me, it would also be a first opportunity to travel outside Iran and get a taste for a life free of the strict rules imposed on women in my country. I could not wait to see Roya in her new surroundings and hear all about her soon-to-be-husband and her new life. I loved hearing her voice on our weekly phone calls, but with my parents standing near me, I rarely had a chance to draw her into more intimate discussions or share what was happening in my own life. I had now been married to Hamid for a couple of years, but I was still living at home with Mom and Dad. Frustrating!

But before I could leave Iran, I needed to get Hamid's written and notarized permission. As my husband, he had control over my movements. I could not leave the country without his express approval.

Thankfully, Hamid agreed. At that time, we were still in love, in spite of occasional clouds, and he knew without a doubt that I would return. The trust between us was solid, even if our strange circumstances caused occasional flare-ups of tension. Ours was not an ordinary marriage, that's for sure.

I was thrilled at the prospect of a change in my routine! I gleefully packed a small suitcase, excited at the prospect of discovering the world beyond our national borders. And if I got my visa, I might spend several weeks with my whole family.

. . .

The trip to Ankara felt like a small party in itself: One of Dad's sisters, her daughter, my cousin and the wife of Dad's youngest brother accompanied us. Many of Dad's relatives had ended up in the US, whereas Mom's opted to settle in Europe, mostly in Sweden and Germany.

As the three youngest members of our small family travel group, my uncle's stunning young wife, my cousin and I wanted to make the most of our stay in Ankara. While my parents and aunt stayed at the hotel, us three would hit the town at night. Stepping out in public without hijab, feeling the breeze on my hair, and being allowed to sit in a bar and have a drink was exhilarating. We welcomed this brief break from the reality of our lives in Tehran. We were young and enjoying harmless fun while our husbands waited for us at home.

The staff at the American embassy in Ankara spoke Farsi very well. Dealing with hundreds of Iranian visa applications daily was one of their main activities and the Embassy had boosted its staff to respond to the deluge of visa requests. Most Iranians who wanted to travel to the US or dealt with legal matters concerning Iranians in the US turned up at the Embassy in Ankara or the US Consulate in Istanbul, as Turkey shared a border with Iran and was one of the rare countries they could travel to without visa.

Outside the secure compound, the American Embassy, people settled for a long wait. Street merchants sold drinks and food, providing sustenance to the crowd. Sitting outside the building, we learned to recognize familiar faces who mingled with the crowd and engaged in conversation with the visa applicants. They were fellow Iranians living in Turkey, who offered assistance to visitors from their home country. They helped them fill out applications and paperwork, made sure their documents were in order, and provided translation if needed—all for a fee, of course. It was a lucrative business. One particular young man among these fixers was known to have connections that enabled him to obtain a visa on the black market for people desperate or wealthy enough to pay a large chunk of money.

On the morning of our appointment at the embassy, I woke up with my heart full of hope. In my mind, there was no reason why the US authorities would deny me a visa. I was married and my husband would remain in Iran, proving that I would not try to overstay illegally after my visa expired. I naively thought this would be sufficient to validate my application for a short visit to attend my sister's wedding.

The United States had welcomed tens of thousands of Iranians as refugees after the revolution. Many people found the living conditions in Iran unbearable under the dictatorial regime of the mullahs and this triggered a massive exodus. Large numbers of people were seeking a way out, and the United States—more specifically Los Angeles—was the preferred destination for most would-be exiles from Iran. Today the city, and more broadly the Southern California region, is home to the biggest population of Iranians outside of Iran—me and numerous members of my direct and extended family included.

By the mid-90s, the US administration was beginning to make it harder for Iranians to visit, even for a short stay. Young single men or women found visas hard to obtain, as this demographic group was viewed as most likely to settle illegally in the US. Unless you had been accepted by a university or sponsored for work by a private sector company, the authorities turned down your request. They did not want too many immigrants marrying Americans to obtain US citizenship.

I thought traveling as a married woman without my significant other would increase my chances. But the list of requirements had grown longer: Owning a house, having a fat bank account, leaving children behind were among the new criteria that I could not meet. I was heartbroken when I was denied a visa while my parents, my aunt and my cousin got theirs. My uncle's young wife, who was not much older than me, also saw her hope of traveling to the US crushed. My parents, on the other hand, had traveled to California several times to visit their children and their record showed that they had always abided by the rules and returned to Iran within the time limit.

A few days later, we all boarded the bus for the long trip back to Tehran. The party was over! My heart was heavy. I had missed Hamid during my stay in Turkey, but less than I had expected. I was returning to life under a repressive regime and a marriage that was official but had yet to be acknowledged by my husband's family, while my parents would prepare for their upcoming trip to California.

I knew my parents were bitterly disappointed too: Roya's wedding would have offered an opportunity to gather all their children in one place for the first time in well over a decade. Political circumstances had blown up our family unit. There were now more of us in the Los Angeles area than in Iran. Still unhappy that my marriage was stuck in a strange limbo, my parents might also have secretly prayed that once I got a taste of life in California with my siblings and cousins, I would choose to enjoy independence on a more permanent basis and turn my back on Hamid.

•   •   •

The following weeks were a whirlwind of preparations for my parents. I was used to them leaving for long periods, but this time was different. Missing Roya's wedding felt painful! Also, the brief taste of life outside Iran had shone a spotlight on my weird existence in Tehran—married, but not living with my husband who still insisted on hiding our relationship.

I felt lonely in advance, and sad that I would be left on my own while the rest of my family was having fun. Hamid spent time with me at my parents' house, but he usually left my room in the late hours to spend the night at his mom's. From the moment we got married, I hated having to sleep and wake up alone without my husband by my side. Now, it had become intolerable.

I put my foot down and demanded that Hamid make our marriage public.

"This is ridiculous, we're married now. We have waited long enough," I said firmly." I don't want to live in this apartment alone by myself while my parents are away."

This time, I got support from my dad who had been uneasy with this situation for a long time. It was not customary for young women to live on their own in Iran—and definitely not in Dad's conservative circles. My father was getting impatient with his son-in-law's inability to confront his mother.

"You need to talk to your mother," he told Hamid. I was delighted that Dad added his weight to my pleas. Our combined pressure eventually produced results.

• • •

I stood by the window, waiting apprehensively for Hamid to appear. When I spotted his approaching figure down the street, I immediately knew his encounter with his mom had gone badly. From his slumping shoulders and the way he dragged his feet, his entire body language shouted "defeat". This was confirmed when he walked in. He had the bewildered gaze of a lost child, adrift and hurt.

"What happened?" I asked. "What did she say?"

Hamid shook his head, sighed deeply and said, "She kicked me out." I then noticed the kitbag he was carrying. He looked on the verge of tears.

"Don't worry, baby. She will come around," I told him with as much confidence as I could muster.

In reality, I was not so sure she would. I wrapped Hamid in a warm embrace while he rested his head on my shoulder. He was upset. I eventually got some details out of him. As I had anticipated, Parvin raised hell about our marriage, and her fury grew worse when she heard we had gone behind her back and tied the knot nearly two years earlier.

"I can't believe you did this to me. How could you?" She yelled maniacally.

"Calm down, mom" Hamid told her. "What is done is done. We want to have a normal life now. Naz's father is on board. Why can't you also be happy for us?"

But his mom would not see sense, Hamid said. She alternated between extreme anger, expressing disparaging opinions about me and my family that my husband refused to share. Then she burst into tears, claiming to be the powerless victim of a world conspiracy.

I did not need further details to picture the scene. My mother-in-law was a selfish woman, a master manipulator who used her widowhood to pull on her children's heartstrings and strengthen her grip over them. But I kept my thoughts to myself. Judging from its impact on Hamid, she must have produced an Oscar-worthy performance.

So, for a few days that were blissful for me, Hamid settled in my parents' apartment and we stopped worrying about his mother. At least, I did. But the relief was short-lived. Within less than a week, Parvin regretted her decision to kick Hamid out and she sent for him.

I had a sense of foreboding when he set off to reconcile with his mom. She had done some thinking, she explained, and realized that Hamid was unlikely to leave me, now that our marriage was official. She understood that if she wanted to see him, she would have to accept me into her life. Parvin showing contrition? I had my doubts. Maybe her retreat was strategic: She was playing a long game and had other plans. Whatever it was, she invited me and my parents over to her house. We would all discuss the situation and figure a sensible way to sort out the current mess.

· · ·

Even when she was making her best efforts to be conciliatory, Parvin could not hide her disdain for me and my parents. She treated us like inferior beings, second-rate citizens who should feel grateful to be allowed in her presence. I never understood why she felt so superior. Her condescending attitude was not limited to us. I later discovered that she also looked down on her husband's brother and his family, who were a friendly, down-to-earth bunch—just like my parents. Unlike her, Hamid's uncle and his family accepted and respected me, and always treated me with kindness.

My parents might not have come from a wealthy family but they were kind and honest people, well respected in the community, who had reached a comfortable position in society through hard work. Hamid's mother had no skills or credentials nor indeed a fancy background to justify her belief that she was a cut above all of us. She was just a snob, whose patronizing attitude had rubbed her husband's side of the family the wrong way, driving a wedge between him and his brother.

At first, I was ready to give Parvin the benefit of the doubt: She was my husband's mother and I knew that Hamid and Pooneh felt very protective of her after her husband's passing. But she did not make it easy for anyone to like her.

For all her delusions that she was a classy lady from the upper tier of society, she did not look like one at all. She was a short, overweight middle-aged woman with a poor dress sense. A bad nose job had left her looking like a witch. The Witch! This seemed an appropriate name for her. Her hair was yellow rather than blond and fried from using bleach too frequently. She did not bother, or could not afford, to maintain her hair color regularly and showed a good amount of gray at the roots. None of this would have mattered if she had shown some warmth, but her cold demeanor only drew attention to her physical flaws. I could not help but feel that the ugliness inside her was showing on the outside, though I kept silent to protect Hamid's feelings.

· · ·

During our time together, Hamid tried his hand at various businesses, but he was always unsuccessful. Parvin's hopes and dreams of getting her son set up for life through marriage into a wealthy family were now shattered for good.

Finding out that we had gone behind her back was a huge shock for her, magnified by her deep sense of betrayal. How many times had I warned Hamid that leaving her in the dark would only make things worse? And, as I also predicted, she could not blame her son, the embodiment of perfection in her eyes. The villain of the story could only be me.

Parvin was a very unhappy woman who felt life had dealt an unfair blow with her husband's sudden demise. Her disheveled state showed that she had given up on life and let herself go. In many ways, she was deserving of compassion, but far from having learned from her tragic change of circumstances and acknowledging that she needed help and support, she raged against her unjust fate and took out her anger on the rest of the world. She was judgmental, often climbing on her high horse to criticize others—me in particular. She justified her meanness by claiming, against all evidence, that royal blood coursed through her veins. Parvin had suffered, but I was fed up with being the target of her unhappiness.

The meeting between our families felt about as friendly as peace talks between adversaries who are forced to sit at the negotiation table at the end of a long conflict. My romance with Hamid was now a commodity, discussed in cold blood between opposing camps. He and I were the main protagonists of our love story, but our parents' intervention had reduced us to secondary characters.

After a couple of hours of back and forth and much haggling, it was decided that we would reset the counter on our marriage, start over and do it right. Parvin agreed to help us find an apartment to rent in a nice neighborhood. My parents, as tradition required, would furnish the place and provide the appliances we needed to set up our household. Within a few days, we found a one-bedroom apartment in a newly built apartment block in the northern, fancier part of the city. The streets were clean and lined with tall green trees and mansions hiding behind imposing gates. Our apartment was small, but it was a nest of our own.

Before leaving to attend Roya's wedding in America, my parents dug into what was left of their savings to equip our little apartment with brand new furniture and appliances. I loved the newness of it all: The building, our furniture and the beginning of our life as a REAL married couple. Deep down, a little voice inside me was telling me that we were only kids playing house. It did not feel like a proper marriage. I was still very young and so was my immature, irresponsible husband. After the ups and downs of the past couple of years, some of the gloss had gone off our relationship.

Still, after playing hide and seek for so long, constantly worried about others finding out—first the authorities, my parents, then his mom—I was overjoyed that Hamid and I could finally settle down independently, in a place of our own. Soon the sadness I felt about missing Roya's wedding was replaced with the excitement of starting this new chapter. Legally, we had already been married for nearly two years, but this was a re-launch, a fresh start in the public eye. Finally, we could let the sun shine on our romance.

Before my parents left, my mom and I rushed around the city to choose the household appliances we needed. We went to the spice market to fill our bare kitchen cabinets. I had always avoided housekeeping chores and never learned to cook. Mom rarely asked me to help in the kitchen when I was a child because I did not enjoy it, although I do remember sitting down with her on the kitchen floor, sorting through piles of herbs from the market that would go into the preparation of succulent dishes.

In a last-minute attempt to turn me into a suitable wife, mom took me to the bazaar and talked me through a few mouthwatering recipes. Pointing to the different kinds of rice piled high on the counters, she showed me which one to use for dolmeh, stuffed vegetables and vine leaves, or which type for chello or pollo. She explained how to cook tahdeeg to produce a golden crust of rice at the bottom of the pans. Decades after I left Iran, I have learned that no other nation on earth cooks rice better than the Persians.

From pots and pans to home decorations, my parents tried to give us everything a young couple needed to start their married life—in fact, far more than we required, to ensure that Hamid's mom could not complain. Even if it stretched their budget beyond what was reasonable, my parents were determined not to appear stingy. The politics of negotiated marriages!

I knew I was a lost cause in the kitchen, but I shadowed my mom for a few days to learn the basics. "Good" wives were expected to produce decent food for their husband. I, too, was weary of Parvin's criticism. I was determined to show her that she was wrong to oppose our union. I knew I could make Hamid happy and was worthy of his love. Now I had to demonstrate it for her.

· · ·

For a few months, we tried to fit the image of a young couple happily embarking on a life together. I kept the house clean and even tried to cook meals for my husband, not always covering myself in glory. Even if I still felt like a kid pretending to be grown up, I was determined to make it work. Most of the time we went out to see friends, relishing our newfound ability to move around, sit together in public and enjoy life as a legally wed couple.

But harsh reality caught up with us. Although far from stupid, Hamid was regularly tripped up by a huge sense of entitlement. He was a college dropout but expected money to flow quickly and freely into his pockets, despite a lack of skills and a reluctance to put in much effort into any endeavor. The few jobs he tried never lasted long because he never tried hard enough.

His attempts at starting businesses faced similar hurdles. Hamid lacked management experience, but unsurprisingly, given his upbringing, the activities that attracted him involved status and luxury, rather than hard graft. For a while, he tried to run a luxury watch business, selling Rolex and Cartier timepieces. There was a big market for status accessories in Tehran, but no retail business gets off the ground without solid work and marketing over a sustained period of time.

But Hamid had no patience—he planted seeds but could neither nurture them nor wait to see them grow. He wanted to pick money from a mature tree.

His inability to succeed meant that we had no income and we struggled to cover the rent and our living expenses. I pleaded with him to let me get another job to help out but his ego and pride would prevent him from allowing me to do so.

My parents were already in the US when Hamid and his mother decided that we should move out of the apartment and live with her. My older sister Niloo was now a US citizen, in a position to sponsor them for a green card, which would save them frequent trips to Turkey to obtain visas when they wanted to visit their children and grandchildren. They decided to apply and stay as long as it took for their requests to be processed. Since I was now living with my husband, there was no need for them to rush back.

Miserable, I packed up my newly purchased dishes, utensils, rugs, bedsheets, and all the brand-new appliances and furniture that my parents had bought for us only six months earlier, tears streaming down my cheeks. My only consolation was that my parents were not in Tehran to witness what felt like a crushing defeat. I could just imagine Dad's look. "I told you this guy was no good!"

Hamid and I transported our belongings to my parents' empty apartment for storage. We knew they would not be back for a while. At least, our possessions would be safe until we could afford an apartment again. I desperately wanted to believe it would not take long. Hamid had changed as his confidence was knocked back by a succession of failures, but part of me still trusted him to find a solution.

After breaking the lease and evacuating our little apartment—our first home—we moved to Parvin's condo and squeezed into my husband's old bedroom. We pushed two twin beds together to make a bed big enough for us both. Framed by a small closet on one side and a table with a TV on the other, it filled most of the space in the small room. A realtor would call it bijou! To me, it felt cramped and I sensed that life was about to get a lot harder.

CHAPTER SEVEN

MEETING THE DEVIL

"Why do you stay in prison when the door is so wide open."
–Rumi

Hamid's attitude flipped after we moved to his mother's house. We were broke, and leaving our little nest had forced him to confront his failings as a provider. Instead of buckling down and finding a job—any job—to earn money, he drowned his wounded ego in alcohol.

For a few short weeks at Parvin's house, we managed to maintain a semblance of normal life despite his worsening mood. We saw a few friends, although many of our closest buddies had left the country by then. I was fond of Hamid's paternal uncle, who had children our own age and a big heart. When we went out with his cousins, who enjoyed our company and treated me as an equal member of their family, my husband briefly reverted to the man I have fallen in love with. Whenever Parvin was not around, Hamid's relatives gave him advice and urged him to treat me better and protect me from his mom. I clung to these moments when my old boyfriend resurfaced. They gave me hope that, once he had found a job, we could move out of Parvin's apartment and resume a life of our own.

But these fleeting moments of optimism vanished the minute we returned to the toxic atmosphere of his mother's place, replaced by hopelessness that washed over me. Whenever Parvin was nearby, I could feel the waves of antagonism she directed at me, so strong that I felt she was punching me in the chest.

Her apartment was spacious, with three bedrooms, but the decor was gaudy, cluttered with old-school renaissance paintings and furniture. It contrasted with the more minimal, modern furnishing at my parents' house. But now, the place was neglected and dirty. Unwashed dishes were piled high in the kitchen sink and huge dust balls floated under the furniture.

Looking back, I wonder how I survived months in the gloomy and hostile atmosphere of my mother-in-law's crumbling condo. I grew up with a mother who faced her share of sorrows, but even in the worst circumstances, Mom remained extremely organized and clean and kept the house spick and span. Following her example, I became a neat freak myself. Parvin and her children, on the other hand, tolerated messy and dirty surroundings. The family could no longer afford home help, and they were too lazy to do the work themselves.

Every day I cleaned our bedroom, determined to keep our private space as orderly as I could. But I could not touch the rest of the apartment for fear of offending my thin-skinned mother-in-law. Living in her place was a lesson on how to remain sane with a greasy kitchen and rusty bath! But it did not take me long to learn that the physical environment I lived in, though repellent, was the least of my worries.

The four of us living under the same roof felt deeply disillusioned, albeit for different reasons. Our little coalition of the unhappy could have turned the tide if we had helped each other. But Parvin dictated the tone and all she wanted was to express resentment—about life, about me and the entire world. When she was not pretending I did not exist, she was throwing jabs at me or making snarky comments. She constantly found new ways to convey her dislike, using any available opportunity to belittle me or my family.

Her animosity was infecting Hamid, who could no longer cope with reality and was numbing his pain and despair with growing quantities of alcohol. His mom's verbal attacks were changing his perception and undermining me in his eyes. Gradually, the venom of her unjust accusations spread through his addled mind, poisoning our relationship.

While pampering her son, Parvin treated me like an unwelcome orphan, a poor relative she had been forced to adopt. Instead of standing up for me, his wife, Hamid sided with his spiteful, malicious mother. His true colors were emerging: He was a mommy's boy. The one thing he was good at was being spoiled by mommy dearest.

I could not expect support from Hamid's sister Pooneh, who was a couple years older than me and had been one of my close friends before she found out that I was going out with her brother. Pooneh, too, was unhappy. She had briefly been married before making an inglorious return to the family home, just like her brother.

When I first met Pooneh, we were still kids. At the time, I prided myself on being a tomboy who preferred running outside rather than playing with Barbies, and Pooneh's boyish style appealed to me. We were kindred spirits. With adolescence, I changed and developed an interest in fashion and makeup and I enjoyed displaying my femininity, although unlike many of my more girly friends, I favored black over pink, and shunned pink, ruffles and bows. Pooneh continued to wear baggy men's clothes. On the plump side like her mom, she walked and behaved like a man, sporting a short haircut. I thought nothing of it back then. In my innocence, I was not even aware of same-sex attraction at the time. I only realized Pooneh was a lesbian a couple of years after Hamid and I got married.

Everything started to make sense: Pooneh always had a crush on some girl in high school. Parvin tried to set her daughter up with suitable guys, but Pooneh never had a boyfriend. At one point, she started taking aerobic classes, not because she wanted to get into shape or for health reasons, but because she was in love with the tall, brunette female instructor. In a country that rejected homosexuality as a form of deviance and expected conformity from all its citizens, particularly women, Pooneh tried to keep her sexual orientation a secret.

To get ahead of rumors and gossip about her daughter, Parvin orchestrated a brief relationship with a willing young man, which swiftly led to marriage. She paid for an elaborate wedding, which took place during the period I was secretly married to Hamid. I was not invited, of course. In any case, the marriage only lasted a few months—shorter even than the bride and groom's dating period— and Pooneh returned to Parvin's apartment, to be bossed around by her domineering mother. By the time I moved in as Hamid's wife, our friendship had entirely broken down. Unable to liberate herself from her mother's powerful grip, Pooneh had adopted the corporate line. Everything that was wrong in their lives was Naz's fault!

· · ·

Every evening, when Hamid got home from wherever he had spent the day—not at work, that's for sure!—he sat on the couch, occupying the spot where his dad conducted his nightly drinking and opium-smoking ritual. Alcohol and drug consumption was likely to have contributed to his father's premature death.

Parvin would gently tell her son off for drinking too much from time to time, but she never confronted him. Nor did she ever tell him to stop wallowing in self-pity and find a job.

Hamid started drinking until the early hours of the morning. Some people mellow with drink; others turn violent. My husband was in the latter category. After finishing an entire bottle of vodka by himself, he turned into a person I could no longer recognize—a monster, really. The sweet, attentive boy I had fallen in love with had disappeared without a trace.

Most nights, he stumbled drunk into our bedroom, woke me up, and made a scene. Initially, he just hurled verbal insults at me, abusing me mentally. Stuck in an apartment that felt like enemy's territory, I was vulnerable but I had some fight left in me. I did not listen passively as he yelled slurs at me. I shouted back, sending the false accusations back to their sender, and fought like a tigress against his unjust accusations. My mood alternated between utter hopelessness and fierce anger. As Hamid's all-consuming resentment evolved into a desire to cause me harm, the situation escalated to the next, horrific stage. Talking back was no longer an option.

•   •   •

Holding my breath in bed, dreading the sound of approaching steps, I braced myself for what was coming. It did not take long before Hamid's drunken brawls turned into brutal, physical fights. Flying into sudden rages, he hit me, thumped me and threw me against the wall. I became his punching bag. His fingers left purplish marks on my throat when he tried to choke me—I wore scarves for days to hide their imprint. He wanted to hurt me, beat me into submission and destroy me physically as well as mentally and emotionally.

When he was in this state, he looked like a man possessed—his eyes turned red, his face flushed with blood and his chest puffed out. Snarling and shouting, he transformed into the Devil himself, and I had nowhere to hide. He would force himself on me, his muscly body easily overpowering me. I still tried to fight him off, but he beat me, hard, then had it his way, leaving me sore and despondent.

When he was done with me, he threw a pillow on the floor and forced me to sleep next to our bed. I was only too happy to comply. Hamid disgusted me and my entire body was revulsed by his touch. I had once longed for his caresses but feeling his hands on me gave me goosebumps and triggered nausea. I wanted to be as far from him as I could. So, I took my pillow, crouched in the corner of the room till morning, weeping silently. If I issued so much as a peep, I was confronted with the Devil's fist again.

My bruised body was screaming in agony, but I was not crying only because of the physical pain caused by the rape and beating. I was also mourning a dream that had suddenly turned into a nightmare, a romance that began like a fairytale and ended up like a horror movie.

"Please, Hamid, stop!" I screamed, "You're hurting me. Please, please, stop!"

My cries resonated throughout the apartment. Thin walls separated our bedroom from Parvin's on the left and Pooneh's on the right. From the safety of their beds, Hamid's mother and sister could hear every blow, sob and desperate plea. But they both chose to turn a deaf ear as Hamid pounded me into a pulp, just as they had ignored earlier nightly rows. Not once did they intervene or knock on our door to check what was going on! And the next day, they both avoided my gaze and pretended all was normal when I showed up at breakfast with a black eye and a collection of bruises in all shades of the rainbow. Daily life at home became so miserable that I barely ate and was getting skinnier by the day. But Parvin did not care. If I ended up being killed by her intoxicated son, I had brought it upon myself. Deep down, I believe she was enjoying my obvious distress.

The next day, having sobered up, Hamid would apologize for his behavior, at least in the early days before he fully embraced his violent and sadistic tendencies.

"I love you," he whimpered, "I don't know what came over me"

He then repeated the pattern after the next bottle of vodka. Vodka, brutal assault, abject apology, vodka, more violence... This sequence evolved into a routine.

During the day, I sat on my bed, listless and dazed. At the slightest noise, my heart raced and my palms turned clammy as anxiety soared. I did not know where to turn for help and felt trapped.

At night, Hamid no longer had to wake me at the end of his drinking sessions. I pretended to be asleep when he walked into the room, but fear kept me alert. My ears were attuned to the slight creak of the opening door and the sound of his breathing. Would he be too drunk to force himself onto me tonight?

By now, I knew I would get no support from the other occupants of the apartment. They would not lift a finger to prevent him killing me. This place was no longer a home. It had become a prison and our bedroom a torture chamber.

.   .   .

When I reached the end of my tether and thought things could not get any worse, Hamid took to drinking during the day as well as at night. Mistreatment became a 24/7 occurrence. He no longer tried to justify himself the next day or promise to stop his abhorrent behavior. Wife abuse had become his favorite hobby and any pretext was good to knock me about. If he did not like the tone of my voice that day, if I looked sad because I longed to see my family, if I saw a friend and was 10 minutes late coming home, I paid the price and got beaten up.

As his alcohol consumption soared, our lives became confined to the apartment. We stopped seeing our friends and his cousins. On the rare occasions when we could not avoid receiving visitors, I concealed my bruises with thick makeup and made small talk, pretending all was well.

Once a week, my parents and Roya called me from California, The Witch would usually pick up the phone and pass it on to me. She could not prevent me from speaking to my family: It would have looked suspicious. But she supervised our conversations. Under her watchful eye, I told tales of marital bliss, claiming everything was fine while struggling to contain the sobs building inside me. The knot in my throat made it hard to get the words out. My heart was broken.

.   .   .

Then came that terrible evening, a turning point in our lives.

I was sitting cross-legged on the bed, watching an Iranian TV series. Hamid had picked a fight earlier that evening and I retreated to the bedroom, eager to avoid a violent confrontation. I thought he had calmed down in the meantime, although he went on drinking. How wrong I was!

When the bedroom door slammed shut, I glanced up at Hamid standing by the bed. That's when I saw the knife in his hand. My eyes grew wide and my heart skipped a beat. In his other hand, he was holding a salt container and a lemon that he put down on the floor.

"Get off the bed, bitch," he hissed, grabbing my arm and dragging me off the bed. I could feel his fingertips digging into my flesh. It hurt!

"Let me go, Hamid!", I said. "What are you doing?"

The next minute, I was on the floor with Hamid sitting in front of me, his legs wrapped tight around my body to prevent me from moving or getting up. We were both wedged in the narrow space between the bed frame and the wall.

With calm, deliberate moves, and a mad look in his eyes, Hamid started carving two-inch cuts on my forearm, all the way down to my wrist. As I felt the sting of the blade, I tried to pull my arm away and break free but the more I fought back, the deeper the knife cut into my flesh. Hamid was strong and his athletic body was three times bigger than my small figure. I could not pull away. He smirked with quiet satisfaction as my tears mixed with the blood dripping from my arm.

When he finished with my left arm, he continued with the right, then rubbed salt and lemons into the bleeding wounds to heighten the pain. In the throes of agony, I lost any sense of reality. Pain was shooting through my body, so intense that I started hyperventilating. I clenched my fists and closed my eyes, overwhelmed by the burning sensation.

Hamid had me securely pinned to the floor. I could not move. I heard screams in the distance, and it took a few moments before I realized they were mine. As I begged him to stop, Hamid laughed. "This is what you deserve" he said with contempt.

His justification for this torture? In his intoxicated state, my husband-turned-monster started ruminating about the past and remembered our first sexual encounter, years ago. "You, bitch," he snarled. "You said you were a virgin, but it was not true. You're a liar!"

Where did that come from? The bleeding at the time was clear evidence that I had never been intimate with a man before. Hamid knew that the baseless accusations would hurt me almost as much as the cuts on my arm. Who knew what went on in his alcohol-infused mind?

Get away from him! My mind was telling me to flee, but I was unable to move. Hamid's volatile temper made him dangerous. I knew that if I tried to argue or deny his accusations, it would further enrage him and things would get much worse. Staring at me with bulging eyes, he was still wielding the lethal weapon. One more word, and he would thrust the knife into me.

So, I sat dejected, my face smeared with tears, and patiently waited for him to pass out. When he finally did, I got up from the blood-soaked carpet, struggled to find my feet and stumbled to the bathroom where I tended to my bleeding wounds. I winced as I cleaned the open cuts with disinfectant. It stung but not as much as the sense of utter despair I felt at that moment.

To this day, the network of thin white scars on my arms is a constant reminder of that terrible night when my relationship with Hamid finally crumbled. We had reached a new low, a point of no return. With absolute clarity, I realized that unless I left soon, my husband would end up killing me. But it would still take a while until I could walk out.

. . .

Sexual, physical and verbal abuse became integral aspects of my daily life. The more frustrated Hamid became about his inability to succeed professionally, the more he directed his anger at me. Hurting me was his way of letting off steam. He sadistically found joy in my pain and would not stop. His mother made no attempt to rein in his worsening behavior. I suspect she quietly approved and enjoyed seeing me suffer. My pain and suffering brought mother and son closer together.

By then, I hated Hamid, I loathed the despicable brute he had become. But most of my anger was directed at my own failures. I blamed myself for not listening to my dad's warnings. Any remnant of love I had ever felt for Hamid was gone. I could not stand the sight of him, but he and his mom exercised strong control over me and my movements. I could see no way out! The fighter in me had gone missing, driven out by the monster that appeared at my door every night. I was paralyzed.

Consumed by fear and self-loathing, I did not tell anyone what was happening. I had little contact with the outside world and no one I could confide in. My parents and siblings were on the other side of the globe, unaware that my marriage had turned into a living hell. Imprisoned within the walls of this condo, I had not seen my friends for months. Nothing mattered anymore. Hamid repelled me and I despised myself for allowing him to control my life.

Day after day, I sat in the apartment in a zombie-like trance, increasingly detached from reality. Our bedroom had become my prison cell, my hell. He was my torturer, and his sister and mother my prison guards.

Hamid was free to flirt with any girl who took his fancy. When friends of his sister's visited, he played the charmer, touching and kissing them in front of me as if I did not exist. Better them than me! I did not want him near me. I would rather be invisible so he could no longer hurt me. Another woman might provide a distraction and keep him away for a while.

One day, I walked in on him fooling around with his youngest cousin, who was around 17 at the time. The scene is etched on my memory. How far my handsome boy had fallen! He was now a debauched drunkard, seeking cheap pleasures to avoid facing his failures. Shocked, I just closed the door, walked away and blocked out what I had just witnessed.

.   .   .

On the rare occasions when Hamid went out with his mom and his sister, I had a few hours on my own in the apartment. Before leaving, they locked me inside the condo and made sure I could not reach out to friends or relatives by disconnecting the phone cables and hiding the phone in a locked closet. They took the key.

They gave the security guard in the lobby instructions not to let me leave the building, in case I somehow managed to escape from the apartment. What excuse did they give to justify such a request? I have no idea. At least, when they were away, I could walk around the entire apartment without feeling malevolent eyes on me all the time. I could also eat on my own—not that I had much appetite, I had lost a lot of weight—and for a few hours, I could breathe without fear.

I needed to get out of this wretched situation. Looking out of the window, I tried to find an escape route, but we were on the 15th floor. Short of jumping to my death, there was no way out. I was at times tempted, but I pictured the sadness on my dad's face and the guilt that my parents would carry for the rest of their lives. Roya, who had saved my life once, would be heartbroken.

But with all my relatives far away, I felt hopeless and helpless. In my dark moments, I was painfully aware that I had insisted on marrying this brute and had chosen to live with him. Maybe this was my punishment for making the wrong choices. With no one to turn to, I had to live with the consequences and accept this inferno as my destiny.

Round and round, thoughts would churn in my head: How could I have failed to see Hamid for the beast he was? How did I, the rebel who yearned to be free, end up in this abusive relationship, a prison of own making? How could I have been so stupid?

It took me many years to come to terms with this traumatic period of my life and stop blaming myself for falling in love with the devil in disguise. I was young and inexperienced at the time. I now better understand the mechanisms of coercive control and the patterns of abusive relationships that prevent women from escaping, sometimes until it is too late. Too many domestic violence survivors blame themselves for the violence inflicted upon them. "Look what you made me do," is a classic excuse that abusers exploit to shift the guilt to their victims. Every day, women around the world are killed by partners who pretend to love them when in reality they want to own them and exercise total power. When abuse occurs, the fault always lies with the perpetrator, not the person at the receiving end. The use of violence is a choice, and no matter how angry they are, abusers always have the option to walk away from a fight rather than let their violent instincts take over.

I now know that you can fall passionately in love with someone without ever seeing the darkness in their soul. Finding a safe path out of a dysfunctional, brutal relationship requires time and bravery.

Over the following weeks, though diminished and battered, the fighter in me tried to raise her voice inside my head. Eventually, her message got through: You alone have the power to break this destructive cycle. Seeking help is an act of courage, a first step toward breaking free.

CHAPTER EIGHT

A DREAM IS BORN

"Have patience. All things are difficult before they become easy."
–Saadi

Locked inside Parvin's apartment, trapped in a marriage to a man I had come to hate, I spent my days staring longingly at pictures of Roya's wedding that my parents had sent me from the United States. Oh, how I missed my family! I dreamed of being with them, released from this bedroom that had turned into a prison.

Whenever my parents called, I sobbed uncontrollably but I never whispered a word about the state of my marriage and the vicious abuse I suffered. I could no longer pretend that I was happy, but I justified my tears by saying that I missed them terribly. They had been away close to a year!

Like a deer caught in headlights, I was crippled by dread and self-blame. After forcing my parents to accept my marriage to Hamid and witnessing the humiliating manner Parvin had treated them, as if they were their inferior rather than equals, part of me accepted that I should suffer the consequences of my mistakes. Thinking about it decades later, I realize that the integrity, respect and compassion that my family showed in all situations made them far better people than this heartless woman disliked by so many. At the time, in spite of this sense of shame, in a small corner of my mind the voice of the rebel I had once been was calling out, "Don't give up! You deserve better!" I needed to regain control of my life.

. . .

The break came on a momentous day when Pooneh and I were home alone. Hamid and his mom had turned to gambling in an attempt to earn some money, and they joined an underground poker game at least once a week. They usually lost and returned home in a filthy mood. I tried to avoid Hamid at all costs on those days.

The phone rang and Pooneh answered.

"It's your sister," she yelled from the other room.

I grabbed the phone from her, went into my room and closed the door behind me to have some privacy. The second I heard Roya's voice, I lost it and collapsed into irrepressible sobs. I was bawling so hard that I could not get a word out.

The night before, I had been beaten badly. My entire body throbbed, and every move re-awakened the pain. I probably weighed a hundred pounds or less. Appetite eluded me and I had not eaten a proper meal in months. I was fragile and weak—broken, physically and emotionally.

When I occasionally caught a glimpse of myself in the mirror, I was shocked by the image it reflected: red and purple bruises, cuts all over my face and body, and dark circles under my sunken eyes. Just as painful and humiliating, but less visible was the raw soreness between my legs caused by violent rape night after night. I hardly recognized myself. Every day, I wondered if I was going to survive, but I did not even care. Surely death would not be worse than what I experienced daily.

My agitated state alarmed Roya. "What is wrong? Tell me," she kept asking. "Talk to me. Has anything happened?" She knew me as her tough little sister, emotionally strong, and did not believe for an instant that missing my family could cause such distress. I heard the concern in her voice.

It took several minutes until I could compose myself enough to talk. The story of the past few months was blurted out by me after I finally caved in. Hamid's drunken outbursts, the verbal abuse and daily insults I suffered from him and his mother, the crescendo of physical violence and the brutal nightly sexual assaults. I told her about getting choked until I nearly fainted and thrown against the wall. As I unveiled the catalogue of horrors Hamid had subjected me to, I left out the traumatic instance when Hamid cold-bloodedly cut my arms as I felt it might be too much for Roya to handle at the moment. My broken body could not withstand much more, I told my sister. Months of pent-up emotions spilled out of me.

Years later, my sister told me that my account of Hamid's ill treatment left her so overwhelmed by shock, followed by mounting rage, that after the first few minutes, she could no longer hear anything. She did not even hear half of the barbaric ways he sought to harm me. That day, Roya wept quietly at the other end of the line, but she tried to keep her voice calm and composed for my sake.

"I can't leave because they lock me in the apartment," I told Roya. "They even prevent me from using the phone when they're away so I can't reach out for help."

I also explained that my mother-in-law regularly unleashed barrages of cruel words against me and ignored my screams and cries for help. "Please, don't tell Dad," I begged Roya. "He warned me over and over and I didn't listen. He will kill me".

Thinking about it now, I can see that worrying about my father's opinion at such a critical moment was strange. I was far more likely to be killed by Hamid! But worrying about Dad's tempestuous reactions was ingrained in me.

"Don't worry about dad," Roya said before asking, "Why Naz? Why didn't you say something earlier? Why would you put up with this and not tell any of us what was happening?"

I confessed that I was scared and ashamed. I had insisted on marrying this man even when our parents had begged me not to go through with it. My huge mistake caused me deep embarrassment. My parents had noticed that Hamid was weak and did not have enough backbone to stand up to his domineering mother.

"I'm paying for my life choices," I told Roya. My tone of resignation alarmed my sister, who went silent. She was horrified that Hamid's daily attacks had crushed her defiant little sister's spirit to such an extent. She listened intently as I expressed disgust at my own foolishness, then let out a sigh and said, "I will call you back shortly. Stay by the phone."

Thirty minutes later—which felt more like three hours—the phone rang again. Pooneh was still in her room, listening to loud music and probably daydreaming about her fitness instructor. I picked up the phone after the first ring. "Hello?"

It was Roya. "Listen to me carefully. Pack your belongings now and go to Mom and Dad's apartment. Lock the door behind you and hide. Stay there and don't leave the apartment under any circumstances. Don't answer the door," she instructed. "Dad is calling Uncle Ali. He will come to see you at the apartment and make a plan. Stay there until you hear from him."

"But how am I going to get out of this place?" I asked. "Pooneh is in the next room. I have no way of leaving"

"Leave before Parvin and Hamid return. You're a strong and smart girl. I'm sure you can find a way . All will be fine, you'll see."

Roya's steady voice gave me strength. I needed someone to guide me out of my current predicament, and she was doing it! My sister, my guardian angel, was saving my life once more.

In practical terms, nothing had really changed and getting out of Parvin's apartment was still a challenge, but mentally I now felt equipped to take it on. The clear instructions that my sister gave me over the phone, her quiet resolve to get me out of my hopeless situation, and most importantly her belief in me had worked their magic. Stuck in a dark place for a long time, I could now see the light after Roya opened a crack. The little voice inside me that said, "You can do this!" was getting louder.

Despite my pleas for secrecy, Roya had revealed my plight to our parents. Deep in my heart, I knew that my dad would never tolerate what Hamid and his family were doing to me, but I still felt a chill down my back when I thought of facing my parents. The shame! The guilt! I would have to own up to the greatest mistake in my life. It pained me to tell my parents the truth and admit they had been right all along. Was it fear, pride, confusion? Maybe a combination of all of these powerful feelings.

There may have been a cultural element, too. "You reap what you sow along the way," our parents always emphasized, creating a sense of unspoken shame associated with being wrong.

Also, I had grown up in an abusive household. Hamid had reached extremes of cruelty toward me, but I had watched my parents fight since I was a little girl and witnessed how their fights often turned physical. Families provide the lens through which we understand the world. My parents' behavior while I was growing up shaped my understanding of right and wrong.

From early on, I was conditioned to believe that I had to put up with a degree of violence in my marriage because I had seen it happening in my own family from time to time, although never to the extend I experienced at the hands of Hamid. I was not even familiar with the term "domestic abuse." In our traditional community, there were no activists, no advocates to talk about the culture of abuse and how wrong it was to normalize it. In my case, my dad's treatment of my mother and the closed-off environment of Iran where women had few rights had influenced my perception of men and what behavior was acceptable. Of course, I knew that violence was wrong, but blinded by love I convinced myself for a long time that it was not such a big deal.

In the States, domestic abuse is discussed more openly, but walking out and escaping the cycle of violence remains hard for many people, even if support is available.

I needed to dig deep within me to find the energy to take action and reclaim my life. That day, my sister Roya helped restore my faith in myself. She unlocked the mental door that enabled me to escape.

•   •   •

Bolstered by Roya's quiet words, I mustered what was left of my emotional strength to pack up and get the hell out of there.

I had to plan my escape. Pooneh was still in her room. She had not been supportive in recent months and mostly ignored me, but she was not as evil and unreasonable as her mother and brother. We also had a history of friendship that went back to our childhood.

Packing my few belongings did not take long since I had not brought much to this apartment. While gathering my stuff, I rehearsed in my head what I was going to tell Pooneh.

In front of my bedroom door, bag in hand, I took a deep breath. Time for action! I stepped out and walked decisively toward the exit, pausing in front of Pooneh's bedroom. There was no way I could get past without her noticing. I would have to talk my way out.

My sister-in-law was reading a book with music blaring in the background. She looked up, surprised to see me standing there in my outdoor clothes, holding a small suitcase. She opened her mouth, but before she could ask her question, I blurted out the few sentences I had prepared.

"You must have noticed that things are really bad between me and your brother at the moment. He beats me every night when he is drunk. I'm sure you have heard me cry and beg him to stop," I said. "I need a few days apart from him to get myself together and give him time to miss me, so we can get back on track."

Tears welled up while I spoke and were now rolling down my face. I could not hold it together anymore.

Shocked and confused, Pooneh asked:" Where are you going?"

"To my uncle's, just for a couple of days. Please, please, please. I am begging you, let me go. For the future of our marriage." Obviously, saving my marriage was no longer an option. I was way past thinking of a future with Hamid the point and had no intention of ever coming back. But I had to get past her defenses.

My sister-in-law was afraid, I sensed it. Hamid would be furious with her and so would her mother if she let me go. But, deep down, she was still a more decent being that the other members of her family. Seeing me standing in front of her, battered and broken, and begging for help, shook her. She took pity on me.

" Ok..." she said reluctantly, "but what am I supposed to tell Hamid and my Mom?"

"Tell them I walked out while you were in the shower," I replied. "You haven't seen me, we haven't spoken."

She hesitated for a few seconds before walking to the door and unlocking it.

With a thankful nod, I walked out of the apartment, overjoyed and overwhelmed, as if I had just been released from maximum-security prison. The elevator took only a minute or so to get to the ground floor, but it felt like a long journey. My heart was jumping out of my chest. Panic set in as I imagined getting caught before having the chance to leave the building. I was petrified.

Before venturing into the open lobby, I hid behind the wall and scanned the area. The security guard was indulging in his daily gossip about the neighbors with one of his maintenance buddies. It kept him busy.

While the two men were distracted, I quietly slipped past the front desk and out into the street. Outside, I took a deep breath. I did not want to risk waiting for a cab in front of the building, so I started running down the street, trying to put as much distance as I could between me and my former prison.

Gripping my small suitcase, I pushed aside anyone on the crowded sidewalk who happened to be in my way without so much as a "sorry". I kept going as fast as I could. Rain was falling, but I didn't worry about getting wet. I looked straight ahead, focused on getting away.

When I was far enough from Hamid's home to feel safer, I stopped, completely out of breath, and hailed a cab. I breathed a sigh of relief as the car sped away, leaving the neighborhood. Thankfully I had enough money left in my wallet to pay for the short cab ride.

I had just left my marriage and felt like a fugitive—as fearful as if I was fleeing law enforcement. In a way, I was. The legislation in Iran gave me no right to leave my husband.

· · ·

Years later, after spending more than fifteen years in the US, I got a friend request on social media. When I clicked to see who had submitted it, I was surprised to discover it was Pooneh. I did not want to friend her and denied her request right away. But by then, I no longer felt resentful of Pooneh and I recognized that she had played a key role in my escape.

I heard, through the grapevine, that she had finally come out as gay and was living the life she wanted. She must have suffered every day for denying her true self for so many years—not just because the Islamic regime condemned homosexuality, but because of the judgement of the close-minded people around her, her mother first and foremost.

Pooneh could only reveal her true self after her mom passed away. Illegal in Iran, same-sex relationships were never discussed nor accepted in the society. They remain largely taboo! After living in California for twenty-five years, I have more gay friends than I can count, and I am proud of each and every one of them for their bravery, living their authentic lives.

· · ·

When I reached my parents' apartment, I unlocked the door with shaky hands, rushed inside and slammed it behind me. I made sure everything was double-locked and bolted, then leaned against the door. With the curtains drawn, the rooms were dark but I could feel the tension in my body receding as I breathed in the familiar smells. I was home!

In the past, this place had not always been the perfect home; but now it was my shelter, my safe haven—a place where Hamid could not lay his hands on me. That was all I needed at that moment.

I wished my parents were there to provide emotional support, but it was not clear when they would be able to come back. The wheels of US bureaucracy turned slowly and their green cards had not yet been granted. I would have to wait for their return.

Once the adrenaline subsided and my stomach no longer felt like it was in my throat, I started settling in. I rearranged some of the furniture to make it easier to move around. To save on storage, Hamid and I all dumped all our furniture and belongings, everything my parents had purchased for us, in my parents' apartment. Two couches, two fridges, two stoves, an extra bed, two dining tables and a pair of every household goods were crammed into the limited space.

I looked around and felt an overwhelming sadness, as well as embarrassment: My parents had spent so much money buying us these items. To give us a good start as a young couple, they had purchased the best appliances they could find. But Hamid and I failed. Material possessions, it turned out, were not an adequate measure of marital success. Looking at the discarded pieces of furniture, I saw the ruins of my life, my hopes and my dreams. Maybe we could sell our possessions second-hand, pass them on to happier couples and recoup some of the money.

• • •

Roya and I set up an elaborate communication system. The phone would ring once, then she hung up and called right back. Then I knew it was safe to answer. Cell phones or caller ID had not reached Iran yet, so we had to come up with creative ways.

It was crucial that Hamid thought I was staying with relatives, surrounded by people who could protect me. He must not know that I was vulnerable, alone in my parents' home. Roya and I agreed a similar code for the doorbell, ahead of my uncle's visit. Later that night, as requested by my dad, Uncle Ali came over to check that all was well. He brought fresh groceries, food and some cash to last me for a week and promised he would take care of Hamid if he ever came looking for me.

The next day, as expected, Hamid called my uncle demanding to speak to me. I was pleased to hear that Pooneh had duly swallowed, and passed on, the lie that I had fed her. Uncle Ali told my husband that I did not want to talk to him, and he should not count on me coming back anytime soon. I needed space and I needed time.

That made Hamid very angry, but my uncle, like my dad, was a strong and confident man who could not be intimidated. Uncle Ali was an educated and worldly man, less old-school and narrow-minded than my dad and their other siblings.

Being the youngest son and second youngest of my grandparents' ten children, he had enjoyed better opportunities than his brothers and sisters and was more sophisticated as a result. He had traveled overseas, received higher education and landed a respectable job. He was also an avid tennis player. His son, my cousin, later became one of Iran's best tennis players and remained a national champion until he left the country, several years after I did and joined us here in Southern California.

Compared to my uncle—and indeed most men—Hamid was a weakling, a loser who had never developed mental strength and character. No matter how many times he called or threatened my uncle, he could not scare him.

·   ·   ·

Days went by. In silence and darkness, I crept around my parents' vacant apartment, making sure outsiders could detect no sign of life. Cooped up at home, I passed the time watching TV with the volume so low that I could barely hear. I read books in semi-darkness with the shades drawn so no one could see inside. I never turned the lights on at night. Only a handful of people knew of my whereabouts, including Mona, my best friend from childhood, and our next-door neighbor who was like a trusted family member.

After a couple of weeks, the phone and the doorbell started ringing at all hours of the day and night. It was Hamid, probably drunk on vodka as he madly pushed the intercom buttons downstairs at 2 am, 3 am and 4 am. My parents' flat sounded like a call center from hell. Each time I heard that shrill ring, it sent a chill of terror down my spine.

Getting no answer from my uncle, Hamid had begun to suspect that I was hiding in my parents 'apartment. He was not prepared to let go. The doors were firmly locked and windows shut, but his manic behavior would still terrorize me. I remained curled up in a ball behind the couch long after the buzzer had gone silent. I was terrified that Hamid could find his way into the apartment. Like when I lived in Parvin's apartment, fear kept me up at night.

Hamid's daily tantrums on my doorstep lasted a few scary weeks. I could not leave the house and did not have the option of calling the police for help.

Here, in the United States, stalking is a crime and prohibited by law. The legislation and enforcement are not perfect, but they do offer some protection if you report such incidents. Repeat perpetrators can even be slammed with restraining orders that bar them from approaching their target's house. From where I stood in Tehran, such rules seemed a luxury.

Back home in Iran, especially after the revolution, running away from my marriage would have made ME the offender, no matter what my husband did to me. If I called the police and asked for protection from domestic abuse, they would handcuff me and force me to go back to my husband and master, probably laughing at me while doing it, too.

Women had no rights in the eyes of the regime. Nearly a quarter of a century after I left, this is still the case. Justice was not available for women in situations like mine. Sharia law dictates that disobeying your husband and defying his wishes is a punishable crime.

After I arrived in the US, I pushed Hamid out of my mind and did my best to forget about him. To a large extent, I succeeded. Years later, I learned through friends that, far from improving after my departure, as his mother had anticipated, Hamid's life spiraled out of control. I am not religious in the traditional sense, more of a spiritual person. I believe that heaven and hell can both be found on this earth. People reap the consequences of what they do, whether good or bad. Karma!

· · ·

Hamid eventually gave up on finding me at my parents' place. Maybe he thought I was out of the country. The doorbell stopped buzzing and the phone only rang when my relatives called. I was feeling a little safer and began to loosen up a bit.

After spending so much time inside, I was suffocating. It had been months since I went outdoors and felt the sun on my skin, so I started stepping out for very short periods of time, first just to get some fresh air in the courtyard of my building. When I grew more confident, I ventured a bit further out and went grocery shopping—all the time looking around me to make sure no one was following me. It was risky, but necessary for my sanity.

One day, my best friend Mona, like me a creative obsessed with old Hollywood movies, came to visit. As we discussed films and theater over a cup of freshly brewed tea, she mentioned that she met someone who could give her access to the set of one of my favorite TV shows.

I was thrilled. My love of film and TV was even stronger than my fear of being discovered by Hamid or his family. I asked Mona if she would take me with her.

"Are you sure it is safe, Naz?" she asked.

"Yes, Hamid has given up on stalking me. I feel a little safer now and I really need something to enjoy after the hell of the last year," I told her.

. . .

My parents' apartment building had two entrances. One at the back of the building opened onto an alley that led to Vali-e-Asr, one of the busiest and longest streets in Tehran. Jammed with heavy traffic and crowds walking on the sidewalk, the avenue was previously called Pahlavi, named after the Shah and his dynasty, overthrown by the revolution. The old name was still frequently used by those who didn't support the revolutionary regime. The front entrance of the building faced a quieter street called Gandhi. It was in a nice neighborhood with less foot traffic. Several foreign embassies were located in the vicinity.

A few days after our conversation, Mona picked me up from the front entrance where traffic was lighter and we were less likely to be spotted by onlookers. I jumped into her car and we headed to the set of a popular TV show starring Khosro Shakibai, one of my all-time favorite actors.

On set, we were greeted by the producer who knew Mona and we were given a tour of the premises. The crew was getting ready to film a scene. As the actors came on and cameras started rolling, I watched, entranced. For the first time, I was witnessing the magic of filmmaking in real time from up close!

Observing the wardrobe people rushing around, the makeup artists touching up the actors' faces between takes and the sound and camera people checking their equipment, I relished the atmosphere on the set. The crew and the cast were all working collectively to create the entertainment that unfolded seamlessly on my TV screens every night. I desperately wanted to be one of them.

After the scene was captured, I made my way to the makeup station and hesitantly introduced myself to the tall, beautiful woman who was head of makeup for the show. I complimented her work and summoned enough courage to say," I love being on set. I would love to work for you! Would you take me on as an assistant? You wouldn't even have to pay me; I just want to learn from you."

She looked at me while cleaning up her brushes and asked,

" Have you ever done makeup before?"

" No, but I love makeup and I practice on myself all the time. I'm a quick learner. If you just give me a chance, you'll see for yourself." I had not really thought it through. Could I even get a job that required leaving the safety of my home every day? Being on set was such an uplifting experience that I was willing to take a chance.

She smiled and replied, "I don't have room for anyone on this show but leave me your phone number and I'll call you if anything comes up."

Thrilled that she had not dismissed my request with a hard "no", I wrote my name and number on a piece of paper, handed it to her and left.

A week later, while sitting in the darkened living room, I received a message on the answering machine. The makeup artist had a new project and needed help. I called her back immediately, apologized for missing her call, and listened to her offer.

" Ok Naz, I got hired to do makeup for a made-for-TV movie that will start filming next week," she told me. "I can't do it because I have to stay on the set of this TV show, which won't complete filming for another two months. Do you want to do the movie?"

I listened, unable to comprehend what she was asking.

"Do what?" I asked.

" The makeup... for the film," she said.

I was confused. " You mean, all by myself? Without your supervision?"

"Yes," she said. "You can come here this week and I'll train you. I can show you how to create each of the character's makeup. It's very simple. No special effects or anything too complicated."

This was an amazing opportunity! If I ever wanted a shot at working in this business, I had to grab it, even with no prior training or work experience on a film set. Thrilled and taken aback in equal measure, I said as casually as I could, "Of course I'll do it, thank you so much for trusting me."

"Ok, good," she replied. "Be here tomorrow at 8:00 AM sharp so we can go over the script and start the training."

"I'll be there," I answered enthusiastically. "May I ask who plays in this film?"

" Kamand Amir-Soleymani and Amin Hayai are the leads," she responded.

I froze! Those were two of the biggest young stars in Iran's film and TV industry at the time.

" Is there a problem?" she asked after an awkward silence.

" No, not at all. I'll be there first thing in the morning."

" Oh, one more thing," she said. "I can't pay you. I am sure you understand. You have no experience and I am taking a big risk putting you in charge."

"Yes, I completely understand. Thank you for the opportunity. I won't let you down."

I hung up the phone and sat still for a while wondering how I would pull this off.

The week of training went by quickly. The makeup artist taught me the basics and went over the makeup required for each of the characters in the movie I would work on.

On my first day on the film set, I was beyond intimidated, especially when I first met the celebrities who starred in the movie. But I got introduced to the cast and crew and rapidly settled in. Every morning a car would pick me up, drive me to the set, and I would get dropped off at home after a day of shooting—all part of the service available to cast and crew. This minimized the risk that I would be spotted by Hamid or anyone close to him.

I became fast friends with both lead actors who, like me, were in their early twenties. I even made it as an extra in one of the scenes. The movie wrapped in a couple of months, far too soon for my liking. I enjoyed every single day on set and never wanted it to end.

For the first time ever, I worked in a field that made me feel alive and fulfilled. Plus, I did a decent job on the makeup part. Kamand, the daughter of a famous actor and herself already a well-known actress, guided me and helped me develop my makeup skills. Working in the film industry since childhood, she had learned how to best enhance her features and hide her minor flaws. Generous and gracious, she never made me feel bad about my lack of skills and experience. On the contrary, she praised my efforts, giving me a confidence boost.

I did not receive a single penny for my work and my name did not appear in the movie credits. Instead, the makeup artist who had hired me was credited for my work. But being invisible did not diminish my happiness and joy. I had worked long hours for no material gain, but my sense of fulfillment was worth a lot. This experience confirmed my passion for the world of movies. It planted a seed that continue to blossom throughout my life.

CHAPTER NINE

CITY OF TWO CONTINENTS

"Whoever has no patience has no wisdom."
–Saadi

When my parents returned to Tehran, having obtained their US green card, my dad called Hamid and asked for a meeting.

After Roya told them everything I had gone through, Mom and Dad were relieved to find me in one piece. I had expected my father to say, "I told you so", but he never referred to the warnings he had given me before I married Hamid.

We hoped that my drunkard husband had come to his senses and would do the right thing: Grant me a divorce. Much as my conservative parents believed in marriage for life, they accepted it was the only way. We thought that if my dad contacted Hamid and asked him man-to-man to end the marriage, he was more likely to respond rationally than if I was involved. Besides, I could not face seeing him, even with Dad by my side.

That morning, my father and Hamid met for a chat in the park right across from Hamid's mom's apartment. Quietly, in a civil manner, my father tried to reason with Hamid and convince him that going our separate ways was the best option. He calmly explained that the way Hamid had treated me was unacceptable, emphasizing that by abusing me, he had irretrievably damaged our relationship while also breaking Dad's trust. When my parents left for the States, Dad had relied on my husband to keep his youngest daughter safe. This meant a lot in our culture. I did wonder if Dad ever reflected on his own attitude toward Mom while talking to my husband, but I was grateful that he was protecting me.

As I suspected, Hamid categorically rejected my dad's suggestion. "Absolutely not. I won't grant a divorce." Hamid wanted me back. I belonged to him. No matter how hard my dad tried, Hamid's answer was an unrelenting "no."

My dad pushed more aggressively. No more mister nice guy... But Hamid did not even blink an eye. His answer remained the same, "Not a chance."

He had the law on his side and knew it. In Iran's fundamentalist Islamic Republic, a husband has the right to deny his wife a divorce, and there is absolutely nothing the woman can do. Conversely, a husband can get rid of his wife just as easily, absolving himself of all responsibility for her upkeep and leaving her with nothing.

In short, I had no legal right to leave my husband and I could not obtain a divorce if he opposed it. Because I was in the wrong in the eyes of the law, Hamid could drag me back if he ever got his hands on me. I had no way out of this marriage.

Over the following weeks, Dad and Uncle Ali made several attempts to convince my husband to set me free. Nothing worked.

It was time to change their approach. My dad tried to bribe him, to threaten him, to intimidate and scare him...all to no avail. Hamid the Weak only felt strong about one thing: I was his property and he would not release me. Not now, not ever!

Eventually, I decided to take matters in my own hands. Maybe if I talked to him, maybe if Hamid heard from me directly that I no longer loved him and would never go back to him, maybe, JUST maybe, he would change his mind.

The thought of talking to Hamid made me shiver. It was terrifying! I took a deep breath, made sure my parents were nearby to give me strength and picked up the phone. The sound of his voice brought back terrible memories, but I tried to be amicable and maintained a soft tone of voice. Or tried to.

Within minutes, I was reduced to pleading and begging him. We spoke for about 30 minutes, covering the same ground over and over, but I achieved nothing at all. In a cold-blooded tone that could not hide the boiling rage bubbling inside him, Hamid gave me his definitive answer. "You can wait until your hair is the color of your teeth, but I won't divorce you." I was devastated. He continued, "You can't hide forever. I will haul you back with my bare hands," before hanging up.

I sat for a long time, barely able to breathe as if Hamid had swung at me with his fist once again. Looking at my parents sitting at the dining table near me, I shook my head in despair. The sense of hopelessness was overwhelming. Would I be stuck for the rest of my life, forever unable to escape my marriage? I had physically escaped his prison, but I was still a fugitive. Mentally and legally, Hamid still had a strong grip on me and I could not shake him off. But I did not want to hide in my parent's apartment until my hair turned as white as my teeth. We had to find another solution!

.　　.　　.

Weeks went by when nothing happened. I was stuck in a holding pattern. At least, my parents were back and provided support, but I was still largely confined to the house, although I occasionally stepped out in their company.

One night, while I was chatting on the phone with Roya, filling her in on the absence of progress, she came up with an idea.

"Why don't you get out of the country and go to Turkey? Pack your bags and leave before Hamid does something stupid," she warned. "This man will stop at nothing to find you and when he does, he will harm you. Just leave Iran. It is not safe for you to stay there any longer."

I did not need a reminder, but Roya pointed out, once more, that if Hamid decided to involve the authorities, I risked being forcibly returned to my husband. He had not done it so far, but how much longer would he wait?

"I agree with everything you said, Roya, but it will never work. How can I get out? I need his written permission to leave the country," I replied.

"Oh, right..." Roya replied, briefly defeated.

After a few minutes of silence, my dad chimed in, sounding upbeat.

"Remember? Hamid signed a permission slip when we traveled to Turkey. We should check. Maybe it's still valid."

I saw a glimmer of hope in my dad's bright blue eyes.

"What if it hasn't expired yet?"

I noted that it was unlikely. Roya's wedding had taken place the year before. But it was worth finding out. My dad and I would go downtown and visit the relevant government agency to find out.

I was not optimistic as we drove to that office the next morning. Hamid knew that many of my family members lived in California and I longed to join them. Canceling the authorization he had given for me to leave the country must have been high on his priority list after I left him. It was the surest way to ensure I could never escape beyond Iran's borders. But we had to knock on all doors in search of a way out.

After waiting patiently in a long queue in a derelict and crowded office building, Dad and I submitted our papers to an agent with a long black beard and beady eyes. He did not look like the type of man who would approve of a wife attempting to leave her husband. As he sifted through files and piles of papers, Dad and I anxiously waited with our best poker faces on. We tried very hard not to show how tense we felt. After finding the relevant record, the functionary looked at my dad—not at me, I was only a woman—and said, "She is still allowed to leave the country. The permit won't expire for another two months." He handed us a copy of the document.

Relief flooded through me. "Don't smile, don't look too happy", I told myself. I couldn't believe what I had just heard. Was it possible that Hamid forgot about the permit? did he think it had already expired? Who cared! For the first time in months, I felt more optimistic about the future.

My dad thanked the man and grabbed my arm tightly as we ran to the car. We hurried home and called Roya right away.

My ever-efficient sister already had a plan in place after staying up all night with husband Rick, plotting my escape. "Pack everything now, leave the country tonight", she insisted, overjoyed that I had the required document.

"Tonight?!" I asked, incredulous.

After reflecting for a few minutes and discussing it with my parents, I realized Roya was right. There was no time to lose. Anything could happen while I remained in Iran. But my relief was tempered by the thought of leaving my home city and the safety of my parents 'place. I could reach Turkey but I had no idea how I could continue my journey. However, I could not afford to hesitate or look back. I had to face the future.

My parents and I swung into action, calling airlines and travel agencies to find a plane ticket. It was the middle of summer and the tourist season was in full flow. Tens of thousands of Iranians vacationed in Turkey every year since it was the closest country where they could enjoy a break free of the Islamic government's restrictions and no visa was required.

"There's no way we can get a seat. There are few flights out of Tehran and no seat is free until next week at the earliest," I said after several unsuccessful attempts. "Then get on a bus, go by ground transportation" Roya suggested when we spoke on the phone.

My dad added: "Yes, it should be easier to find a seat on a bus." My father knew there were far more bus connections between Iran and Turkey planes. As the former owner of a ground transport company, he had himself driven to and from Turkey on many occasions. So, he left the house to purchase tickets and returned shortly afterwards with a reservation for two seats on a bus to Istanbul leaving Tehran the next evening.

We chose Istanbul, rather than the Turkish capital, Ankara, because our next-door neighbor, the garment trader, knew the city very well. She always stayed at the same hotel and had a few contacts there who could help us.

That night, I was restless and did not sleep a wink. The enormity of what I was about to do hit me. Thoughts of leaving my home, my city, my country, possibly forever, were swirling around my head, unsettling me. Iran had been my entire universe so far. In my imagination, I often wandered beyond the frontiers of my native country to escape its constraints. Now I would be doing it for real, leaving the familiar behind to plunge into the unknown. At least, I would be safe from Hamid's abuse.

$$\cdot \quad \cdot \quad \cdot$$

When the sun finally came up, I jumped out of bed and finished packing. I managed to fit everything I needed to take with me into one suitcase. I wanted to travel light in case the journey proved difficult. Reaching Istanbul would be an important first step, but it was only the initial leg of a long journey to the United States. How I would reach my destination was still uncertain.

As the departure time inched closer, I looked at my mother, who was about to say goodbye to another one of her children—the last one. She was not just a mother sending her child off to college and facing an empty nest: One by one,

Mom had been forced to send her children out of the country to save them. The sorrow and concern written on her face mirrored my own thoughts.

"Mom... I haven't said goodbye to any of my friends or to Grandma. She doesn't even know I am leaving." She smiled sadly and said, "There is no time, Naz. I will tell my mother and your friends that you thought of them. Under the circumstances, I'm sure they will understand."

·   ·   ·

Unfortunately, my maternal Grandma passed away a year later and I never had a chance to tell her how much she meant to me. The sorrow of leaving without seeing her one last time weighed on my mind for a long time. I was never close to my dad's parents, but my maternal grandmother had spent a lot of time with us during my childhood. I always enjoyed when she came to stay with us for a few days. She was a kind, pious woman who had endless stories to tell and wisdom to share. She was widowed at a young age and all she had left was her daughters and grandkids. I loved her, and often wondered what she thought of my sudden departure.

·   ·   ·

When the time came for my dad and I to leave, I hugged my mom tightly. I could read her anxiety in her eyes. Her youngest daughter had never traveled alone within Iran's borders, let alone to another country where we knew no one, and Mom's concern was obvious. But she was also relieved that I was finding a way out of a terrible situation and would soon be on my way to a better life. She never had much choice—her path was chosen for her. She wanted me to live freely and be an independent woman. She did not want me to suffer anyone. My pain was her pain.

We both broke down. She was scared for me, and I was frightened too. Many conflicting emotions were running through my head. Would I ever see my mom again? Would she stay alive long enough to see me again? What dangers awaited me on my adventurous journey?

After my departure, she and my dad would be left all alone in Tehran—all their children gone. But it was getting late and we had to leave without delay if we wanted to catch our bus. The time for second guesses had long passed.

At that precise moment, I was too absorbed with my own struggle and the uncertain journey ahead of me to properly express my gratitude to my mom. Inside her was a broken child, married too young, who had suffered and never healed. It would take a couple of decades and long mother-and-daughter conversations in the relaxed atmosphere of Southern California until I could thank her and tell her that I understood and loved her. After experiencing many ups and downs in my own life, I was able to reach out to the child within her and tell her, "I see you."

. . .

As we drove through the city, I tried to take in as much as I could, imprinting its landmarks and smells in my memory. I was not sure when I would see Tehran again, if ever. At the city's bustling ground transportation station, we found our bus, handed our bags to the driver who place them in the compartment below the vehicle, and settled in for what would be a very long journey lasting a little over 30 hours.

The bus left on time and we headed northwest in the direction of Tabriz, the capital of Iran's Azeri province. There, the majority of the population spoke Azeri, a language close to Turkish, rather than Farsi.

I still worried that there would be a last-minute setback that would prevent me from leaving the country. Every time the bus stopped on the way to the Turkish border, I was seized with fear. I was obsessed with the thought that Hamid had found out I was fleeing. "What if he is following us? What if he stops us before we cross the border? What if he had canceled my exit permit and the authorities arrested me before I left Iranian territory? What if he knew that I was escaping and he had informed officials?" I knew my fears were probably unfounded, but I felt restless.

Eventually, we reached the Turkish border near Dogubeyazit, under the majestic shadow of Mount Ararat, the mountain where, legend has it, Noah's Ark came to rest. Its snow-capped peak stood above a vast plain at the crossroads between Armenia, Azerbaijan, Iran and Turkey.

At the border, official formalities did not take long since passengers did not need a visa. Still, on the Iranian side, guards checked people's identity papers. When our turn came, the official barely glanced at my exit permit. I was traveling with my dad—a suitable chaperone—and had my husband's permission to travel. Next!

Once in Turkey, the bus stopped at a roadside café for half an hour—an opportunity for us to get some refreshments and visit the bathroom.

The atmosphere was noticeably more relaxed on the bus when we resumed our trip. I was probably not the only person on the bus who had felt anxious about the border crossing. Maybe other passengers were seeking a permanent way out of Iran. Several female travelers were unrecognizable after removing their head coverings and long coats. It was summer and the heat was stifling. I had also shed my hijab and reappeared in a pair of jeans and T-shirt. Although a conservative country, Turkey did not impose Sharia law. Some passengers had bought beer and were drinking on the bus. Alcohol was freely available in Turkey, even if the majority of the population did not drink alcohol.

Now that I had left Iran, my mind turned to new questions. "Would I be safe? Was I doing the right thing? How would I reach the United States?" As we drove on for hours across the bare Anatolian plateau, my mind was abuzz with questions that I could not answer.

.   .   .

Had I known what awaited me on this side of the border, maybe I would have never left. But once we entered Turkish territory, there was no going back. I had made a choice and it was time for me to put my big girl pants on, keep a brave face and show no weakness. I could not share my fears and doubts with my dad. It would only increase his concerns. I wanted to spare him additional stress.

I still felt guilty for having put my parents through a lot already. Now I had to face up to whatever was coming my way. I was blessed with a second chance at gaining freedom and I wasn't going to mess it up.

Both Dad and I dozed off for brief periods during the never-ending journey. Traffic was heavy when we reached Istanbul, a massive metropolis stretching over dozens of kilometers on both sides of the Bosphorus Strait. The bus terminal at Topkapi was even more chaotic that the one in Tehran. It was a jungle of buses coming and going, with thousands of passengers milling around laden with packed bags tied with string and old suitcases.

Once we had retrieved our bags, Dad got us a taxi and gave the driver the address of the hotel we were going to stay, which had been recommended by our neighbor who frequently visited Istanbul for business. She had lived in the unit next to ours in Tehran for so long that she had become an honorary member of the family.

The hotel was located in Aksaray, a commercial hub a few blocks away from the old city with its picturesque mosques, hookah cafés and bazaars. The tourist area nearby attracted backpackers who flocked to Istanbul from all over the world. Dozens of cheap restaurants and grocery stores catered to their needs.

My dad could not stay long in Istanbul. Business beckoned in Tehran. He made sure I was settled into my temporary home and took me on a tour of the neighborhood to show me where I could find everyday necessities and food. We had no idea how long I would be staying in Istanbul, but neither of us expected my visit to last more than a few weeks.

Before he left, my father talked with Tarik, the young Turkish man who managed the front desk. Our neighbor knew him well and found him reliable. A short, skinny man with a dark mustache, Tarik knew a little bit of Persian and a little bit of English and managed to display a dry sense of humor in spite of communication issues. My dad had befriended him during his short stay, and he wanted Tarik to keep an eye on me just in case I needed help. "Please look after my daughter like you would protect your sister," he urged Tarik.

The day my dad was leaving, we stood in front of the hotel entrance, uncertain when we would see each other again. As we hugged goodbye, we tried to contain our tears. I was my father's daughter. We both knew we had to be strong for one another.

Always protective of his family, often overbearing, my dad found it hard to leave me on my own.

It was difficult for my dad to leave me on my own in an unfamiliar country because it was not safe for a young girl. It broke his heart to abandon me to my fate in Istanbul, with no one to guide me through the next stage. But he also knew that at that precise moment, anywhere was safer than Tehran. From now on, he could only provide support from a distance. He would have to trust me to find my way forward.

. . .

Istanbul truly felt like the intersection of West and East. Although still a patriarchal society and not the most progressive country on earth, with high rates of femicide, the Turkey I saw was a country that offered more freedom to women than Iran after the revolution. If you wanted to cover up your hair and skin because of your religion, you were free to do so, but you could also opt not to wear the hijab if you were a non-practicing Muslim or from another religion. I loved being able to leave the hotel and move around without covering up. It was still a foreign concept to me, but a pleasant one that I rapidly grew used to.

I did not hold much hope that the US Consulate would grant me a visa, since they had denied my earlier request when having a husband waiting for me in Iran should have convinced officials that my visit would be temporary. This time, I was a free agent, seeking permanent refuge. The US Consulate, an elegant 19th former Italian-style palazzo was located in the heart of Pera—the former European quarter when Istanbul was still Constantinople, capital of the Ottoman empire— and it processed large numbers of applications—most of them from my compatriots. As I expected, mine was not successful.

Most days, I did not venture very far from the hotel. I was used to bustling Tehran, but Istanbul was an even larger city and a bit intimidating. Also, I did not speak the language. Even in the tourist zone, there were still sketchy alleyways where I did not want to be alone after dark. I mostly stuck to well frequented streets and preferred to observe the vibrant life in the city from a safe distance. I was not yet attuned to the potential dangers of this unfamiliar place.

Over the next weeks, I established a routine for myself. I spent hours every day watching the world go by, sitting by the window of my hotel room and smoking cigarettes. The hotel location was perfect. The dense crowd provided a constantly changing spectacle: Men in business suits hurrying to work, store owners calling in customers, porters pushing carts laden with goods and tourists taking in the sights and scents of this magnificent ancient city.

My inability to communicate properly often led to frustration. I understood it was misplaced. After all, I was in Turkey and should speak their language. They had no obligation to know English or Farsi just to make things more convenient for me or anyone else who visited their country. Tarik and I managed to exchange simple information in our interesting mix of English and Farsi. I learned a few words of Turkish—just enough to get by.

Many Iranians from the north-west region of Iran speak Azeri, a form of Turkish, but born in Tehran in a Farsi-speaking family, I had never learned the language, unlike my father who had picked up Azeri Turkish during his frequent business trips. In fact, few Farsi speakers made the efforts to learn Azeri. For us in

Tehran, learning to speak English well was far more important. It represented the hope of a life in the US or in the UK.

. . .

While I idly passed the time in Istanbul, Roya and her new husband Rick, whom I had never met, were trying every possible way to get me to America. They wrote to the American ambassador in Istanbul, to Senator Barbara Boxer and even to President Bill Clinton, pleading with them to grant me a visa because my life was in danger. They explained how concerned they were about my safety and told them that I was stuck in Istanbul and could not return to Iran. Despite their efforts to get someone's attention, all doors remained closed.

Every week, they sent me money so I could cover my expenses. I lived a simple life, but I still had to pay for my hotel room—the biggest expense—as well as the small amounts of food I ate. Importantly, my weekly allowance enabled me to buy the pack of cigarettes I consumed every day. To calm my nerves, I took up smoking with a vengeance.

. . .

Days turned to weeks then to months. I lost track of time. When I left the hotel, it was usually to buy cigarettes, instead of food, from a neighborhood bodega that had the TV on in the background all day. Not far from my hotel, I paid daily visits to the place. The small screen behind the counter showed Turkish soap operas and music videos day and night. I did not understand much of what they were saying, but it didn't matter because the silence in my hotel room was often unbearable without a TV set to keep myself entertained.

From my window, I was getting to know my little corner of the city and learning about the daily rhythm of the neighborhood. I watched as the shopkeepers opened up for business each morning and looked at the women who strolled around the area. Some of them wore European-style dresses. Others had a more conservative style. I observed groups of young Turks out for a night on the town and how they moved about in their relative freedom, casually interacting with friends of the opposite sex without fear of reprisals, in marked contrast with Tehran where such encounters had to remain discreet for fear of attracting the hostility of the Morality Police.

Watching the vibrant life unfolding in front of the hotel and people freely mingling in the crowd gave me a taste of what my life might be like in the future… if only I had more certainty about where I was going and how I was going to get there. I was playing a waiting game. I remained hyper alert to the opportunities and dangers the city presented to a young woman alone. It was hard and often boring being stuck in a tiny hotel room, but I was accustomed to hiding out.

I became a familiar presence in the hotel. The cleaners, who noticed how much time I spent in my room, brought me magazines discarded by departing guests. Some of them were in languages I could not even identify, but the fashion photos needed no translation.

Although I was now out of Iran, away from my abusive husband, I was still aware that I was sharing the city with tens of thousands of Iranian tourists. Conspicuous as a solitary female guest in that hotel, I did not want to become too visible in the neighborhood in case friends of Hamid's or people who knew him spotted me. Until I was legally settled in the US, I still faced a degree of risk. I did not want to show up on Hamid's radar.

I got through this period of anxious limbo by daydreaming about my future life. My imagination had been a constant and friendly companion since childhood. I was never really bored when I let my creativity run free.

I created stories about the people I watched moving around as they went about their daily business. They provided fuel for the happy endings I told myself. From sunrise to sunset, I dreamed about the moment when I would be reunited with my family. It was easy for me get lost in my cheery thoughts.

Five times a day, this reverie would be interrupted by the jarring calls for prayer over the loudspeakers from the mosque across the street. It was a jolting reminder that I was still in a Muslim country where a young solo woman traveler was regarded with suspicion at best.

But the call to prayer also brought back many memories of early childhood, of a time before religious worship was forced upon us as a way of life. When we were young kids, we viewed religious gatherings as a form of entertainment. We were mesmerized by the golden domes of the mosques, the beautiful, mirrored tiles and the written verses of the Quran inscribed in elegant calligraphy on the walls.

Not far from my hotel, muezzin called the faithful to prayer from the minarets of Istanbul's famed mosques. Some, like Sultanahmet, also known as the Blue Mosque, were major tourist attractions. When I needed to stretch my legs, I sometimes walked through the crowd as far as the beautiful park that separated the Blue Mosque from Haghia Sophia, an old Byzantine basilica, which was another Istanbul landmark. Where the park now stood, horse races were held in Roman times, the oval shape of the Hippodrome still visible to this day. When the call to prayer sounded, I watched as the Muslim men and women rushed to fulfill their religious duty and wondered if they truly believed in their practice or if they were just doing what they were told. How many of them were just followers and not true believers?

• • •

Attempts to get me a visa were not progressing and I was getting worried. Was I trapped, once again?,

The uncertainty was eating at me. I was growing more anxious and agitated by the day. In addition, Tarik, the front desk manager, had developed a crush on me. I'd been in the hotel too long, and he was acting like a fool.

Some days while I was out, he would let himself into my room, sit on my bed with a bouquet of roses in hand and wait for me to get back. He clearly hoped to get me into bed.

I had no hesitation turning him down, but I resented his invasion of my private space. This small hotel room was my only private refuge. As I battled uncertainty, I needed this safe space.

But Tarik was not taking no for an answer. After I repeatedly rejected his propositions, he changed his tune, confessed his love and asked me to consider marrying him. He thought he could convince me to stay in Istanbul and allow him to take care of me for the rest of my life. Sorry, Tarik! Been there, done that! In other circumstances, I would have found his simple mindset and forlorn hope that I would ACTUALLY give up all my hopes and dreams to marry him funny. But I had nowhere else to go and his persistence made my stay in this hotel uncomfortable. It was getting seriously annoying. His behavior was unacceptable. Already under stress, I was losing patience with this pest. My father had trusted him to look out for me, but instead of protecting me from harm, he was turning into a predator himself.

As if Tarik's unwelcome attentions were not enough, I had to deal with Arab businessmen staying at the hotel. They saw me at the hotel restaurant every morning and stared while I ate my breakfast alone. To keep my spending down, I took advantage of the free buffet-style breakfast that the hotel offered to its guests.

This meant eating downstairs in the dining room, rather than ordering room service. Turks tend to eat lavish breakfasts composed of a multitude of dishes, including eggs and cheese, cucumbers, olives and tomatoes, and it was my favorite meal of the day. The food on offer was actually tasty and I looked forward to it each morning—even if my limited appetite was no match for the amounts of food on offer. But with men watching me like predators eyeing their next meal, it became less enjoyable.

It did not take long for them to notice that I was always by myself. After a few days, they started following me to my room. When I noticed I was being tailed, I walked faster, eventually running into my room and locking the door behind me. But they were persistent and showed up at my door in the middle of the night, knocking aggressively and speaking in loud Arabic. Woken up by the noise, I waited until then finally got tired and frustrated, and left me alone.

These incidents triggered unwelcome reminders of the nights when Hamid would show up at my parents' apartment looking for me and violently ringing the doorbell in the middle of the night. As these instances grew more frequent, I felt restless and fearful.

When dark thoughts caught up with me, I considered giving up and going back to Iran. I could not stay in Istanbul forever and the path ahead was still uncertain. I had the paranoid feeling that Tarik would let himself into my room one night while I was asleep or one of these Arab men would break the door down, force their way in or grab me in the hallway. I had heard claims that women went missing in Turkey at alarming rates every year. Whether these were true or not, they had an impact on my frazzled mind.

Terrifying scenarios ran through my head, but I did not share my fears with my family. I tried to be strong and be patient while Roya and Rick sought a way for me to travel to America. I had to choose fight over flight.

CHAPTER TEN

A WOLF IN SHEEP'S CLOTHING

"I wish I could show you when you are lonely or in darkness the astonishing light of your own being."
–Hafiz

On the phone, I spent days brainstorming and discussing every possible scenario with my parents in Tehran and Roya and Rick in California. Having failed to come up with a legal solution, we decided that buying a visa on the black market was the only option available.

From our previous trip to Ankara, my mother had saved the number of one of the fixers hanging outside the US embassy, offering their services to compatriots in need of assistance. Amin had seen me burst into tears when I was denied a visa to attend Roya's wedding, and he had offered to get me one... for a price. But at that time, I was not under heavy pressure to leave Iran, so we had passed on that expensive opportunity.

Now my homework was to contact him and find out how the process worked and how much it would cost to buy a visa on the black market. I called Amin the next day and briefly explained my situation. He sounded friendly and sympathetic to my plight, even offering to travel to Istanbul from Ankara where he lived, so we could meet and discuss possible options in person. "We can find a solution," he assured me.

. . .

A few days later, he turned up in Istanbul. I greeted him in the hotel lobby and we sat down to talk over a cup of tea. Amin was a tall, charming, good-looking man, with sun-kissed skin and straight shaggy hair. He was polite and soft spoken, and his kind demeanor put me at ease. After I explained my situation and we discussed the gritty details, Amin said he would return to Ankara and work on my case from there.

"I'll call you in a few days and tell you how the situation is progressing," he promised. After a long wait, I finally had a glimmer of hope that things would get moving soon—a hint of light at the end of this long and dark tunnel.

So, when he contacted me a couple of days later and informed me that he would not be able to get me a visa to the U.S at this time, my hopes came crashing down again.

"However," Amin said, "I know someone in Istanbul who can get you a visa to Mexico. But it will cost you about 7,000 American dollars."

That was the price we paid for being an Iranian citizen after the revolution: We were not welcomed or wanted in most countries. Once a proud, progressive nation with great relations with western countries, a country rich in culture and history, my country was now an international pariah. Cyrus the Great, first king of ancient Persia, had issued a chapter of human rights as far back as 539 B.C., freeing slaves and proclaiming racial equality, but today, the citizens of his nation were banned from traveling freely to most destinations. Our Iranian passports identified us as extremists or criminals. In reality, as Iranian civilians, we were the main victims of the regime that had forcefully taken over our lives and caused us much suffering.

This discrimination against Iranian citizens made me very angry. I thought it amounted to unfair treatment of my people. I did not choose where I was born, nor had I ever picked the fundamentalist government that was the enemy of democracies around the world. I'd had no say in the revolution and never approved its rules. Yet here I was, paying the price.

After I told Roya about my new predicament, I tried to talk her out of sending me this large sum of money. She made me promise not to do anything rash and to stay put until she had spoken to Rick. They were already sending me money weekly to support my stay in Istanbul and it made me very uneasy. They were newlyweds, perhaps in debt themselves, and I couldn't agree to them spending that kind of money for me. I didn't want to be a burden and a source of financial stress. They were already working hard to get me out of Istanbul and save me from a marriage I had willfully walked into.

I knew they had cut short their long-delayed honeymoon—a road trip around America—and headed home to work on my behalf, deploying great efforts to help me: Rick, who had not even met me, had written letters and made numerous calls to United Nations representatives and officials at the highest level of the US government. So far, with no success.

With each passing day, my hopes of ever leaving Istanbul were fading. I was losing sense of time. Roya finally called to let me know they had sent me the money for the visa to Mexico. "From Mexico, we can get you to California quite easily," she explained. Before I could object, she continued, "This isn't up for debate Naz. We have wired the money already. Period."

"It's way too much money, Roya. We can find another way," I protested. But I had no alternative plan to suggest and my sister was determined to get me out of Turkey as soon as possible. The next day, I called Amin again and told him that he could start putting the wheels in motion. I would have the money for the visa to Mexico in a few days.

The money arrived in Istanbul in the following days and Amin made his way back to Istanbul shortly afterwards. This time, we met in my room so we could discuss the details of this illegal deal with more privacy. He was in touch with the man who would provide the visa and was still trying to set a time and place for us both to meet him. Amin would stay in Istanbul until everything was taken care of and my passport was duly stamped with a visa to Mexico.

"It's going to take a few days to arrange everything," he said. "Don't worry. It's normal. I hope you understand."

After spending months in Istanbul, I could wait a few more days. I was grateful to Amin, who I viewed like an angel sent by God to guide me out of the weird state of limbo I'd been living in for a long time. My goal was firmly in my mind: At long last, I would reunite with my siblings and start a new life.

·　　·　　·

While we were waiting for mysterious figures to work their magic in the background, Amin kept me company. He took me out to explore parts of Istanbul that I had not had a chance to discover. Reluctant to stray too far out of the neighborhood where was my hotel was located, I had not seen much of this city, famous for its natural beauty and historical landmarks.

Amin picked me up from the hotel in the morning and took me around town. We saw the main tourist attractions like Topkapi Palace, seat of power for generations of Ottoman Sultans, but he also showed me hidden gems that only local knew about. One day, we took a ferry across the Bosphorus to Asia. During the 20-minute crossing, we sat on the side of the boat, watching seagulls dive for fish churned up in its wake. We ate delicious fish and meze—appetizers—in the tiny eateries hidden under the arches of the Galata Bridge, that spans the Golden Horn.

I loved the city's famous centuries-old Bazaar where dozens of jewelers sold gold. In one section of the covered market, windows were full of the kind of shiny bangles that had jingled on my mother's arm. It brought back memories of home. Mom! I missed her. When would I see her again? Tourists and locals mingled in the huge, labyrinthine structure where trade had been conducted for centuries. Beautiful fabrics were piled high in tiny stalls that dated back to the Middle Ages. Amin and I sat on small stools in neighborhood cafés, drinking from thick Turkish coffee from tiny cups. Amin picked up mine and read my fortune from the coffee grounds left at the bottom of my cup. "You will go to the United States," he said pointing to an indistinct shape. I laughed! I wasn't convinced by Amin's fortune-telling routine but I hoped he was right.

We talked about our lives—mine back home and his in Ankara. He had fled Iran during the war because he didn't fight on behalf of a government that he opposed. By now, Turkey had become Amin's home but he knew that, at his core, he would always be Iranian.

I felt relaxed and safe with him, as if he was the boy next door. As anyone who has ever traveled abroad experiences, there is comfort in the easy familiarity that comes from encountering a friendly compatriot, someone who seems to understand exactly where you are coming from.

Amin appeared to care about me and my wellbeing. As we got to know each other over those few days spent waiting and killing time, his friendship rekindled my sense of hope. He promised to get me out of Istanbul and reunite me with my family in the States. I felt I could trust him.

A few days later, a meeting was finally scheduled. We were going to meet the man who could get me a visa to Mexico. That day, Amin came by a little earlier to prep me. He gave me instructions on how to talk and act around the people we were about to meet. Who were they? What was their role? He would not tell me, but I felt I was going to pass an exam.

Hailing a cab in front of the hotel, Amin instructed the driver in fluent Turkish. We were heading to a distant part of town where this mysterious man was waiting for us. Amin could see that I was a bit anxious and he pointed out different monuments and landmarks along the way in an effort to distract me.

After a 30-minute ride, we arrived in a neighborhood that seemed a bit decrepit, sketchy even. But it was too late to change my mind. At this point, I had to rely on Amin. We got out of the cab in front of an old office building and I followed him up a few stairs and into a nondescript office room. I could not figure out what this place was. Was it a government institution? Were the people I was meeting corrupt officials or forgers? Or both? I had no idea. I was no expert on black market operations in Turkey or anywhere else.

This setup seemed as legitimate as any shady business. The shabby room contained several desks with phones and fax machines, a few folders and not much else. Sitting behind one of the desks was a slightly overweight man in his early forties, with a thick dark mustache. He was noisily sipping steaming hot tea from a glass.

The few words of Turkish I had picked up since my arrival in Istanbul were just enough to order food, ask for prices or greet people, but I could not follow the fast exchanges taking place in front of me.

I didn't want to learn Turkish because I wouldn't accept that my stay would be long enough for me to justify learning the language. My stay would have been more permanent if I had become proficient in Turkish. Staying here was not an option! This was an idea that I rejected whenever it crept into my head. I dreaded it!

After a brief conversation with the man, whose name was Murat, Amin formally introduced me. "Merhaba," I told Murat. This was as far as my Turkish would take me. Murat replied politely, and said apologetically, "No English."

Amin suggested that, from now on, he would act as the middleman and take care of all the details. This way, I wouldn't have to travel to this part of town again and deal with strange men I barely understood. I agreed, much relieved. I didn't fully understand why he had even brought me here to meet the man. I could not see what purpose this trip had served. Maybe Murat had wanted to make sure that Amin really had a customer for him. In any case, I was more than willing to let my compatriot handle the matter since he spoke fluent Turkish. I had faith in Amin and it seemed the other party trusted him too.

The two men shook hands: Murat was to start the process immediately and Amin would come back in a few days with the money and my passport, so the visa to Mexico could be stamped into it.

After we returned to the hotel, I started thinking about the trip ahead. I collected a few small gifts I could bring Roya in the following days. I was all set to go!

. . .

The night before Amin was due to pick up my passport, excitement and adrenaline kept me up most of the night. When morning came, I jumped out of my bed, impatient to start the day. It would be a good one! I took a hot shower and got dressed and was ready in the lobby long before the time scheduled for Amin's arrival. When he turned up, we had breakfast together before he headed back to the old office building to get my visa.

I chatted nervously throughout the meal. Amin went over the plan with me one more time. He would take the money and the passport and return within a few hours. I was giddy at the thought of reaching California within days and talked animatedly about all the things I planned to do when I reached my destination. At the back of my mind, there was still a hint of apprehension. It focused mostly on Murat's ability to deliver the visa he had promised. What if something had gone wrong? What if Murat had failed to obtain the visa? But encouraged by Amin who repeatedly assured me that everything would go smoothly, I brushed my concerns aside. After we finished eating, we returned to my room where I'd prepared my passport and a thick envelope containing the money—I had never seen such a large amount in cash!

Tarik, who had seen me meet Amin occasionally, had asked me one day what my connection was with this man. I had a strong urge to tell him this was none of his business, but I kept my composure and said that Amin was an old family friend who had come from Ankara to help me with my travel documents for the embassy. Tarik appeared wary of Amin. Was Tarik's suspicion motivated by jealousy? I didn't know, but he had no right to interfere.

I knew in my heart that handing out my passport and thousands of dollars to a man I'd only known for a few weeks was very risky. But I had no other option. Also, I felt I'd got to know Amin over the past few weeks and I trusted his intentions to help a fellow Iranian on the run. However, my father's last words to me when he left Istanbul were still ringing in my ears:

"It's a dangerous world, Naz. Trust no one."

Now that time had come to hand over my passport and thousands of dollars, Amin could see that conflicting thoughts were running through my head. He saw the fear in my eyes and sensed my tension. This whole process was a crazy venture, I knew it.

Dad's warning was ringing in my head and I knew he was right. But I faced an unenviable choice between two bad options: either take a leap of faith or do nothing at all. Either way, so much was at stake—Roya and Rick's savings, but also my future life.

It pained me to hand over a sum that amounted to Roya and Rick's entire life savings. They had spent most of their resources on their wedding and honeymoon. This money was probably all they had left.

The look on my face said it all: fear, reluctance, regret, but also hope. To overcome my last-minute hesitations, Amin took my hand in his. He looked me in the eye, and in a calm, sweet voice, assured me that everything was going to be alright.

"In a matter of days, you will be with your family" he said confidently, "Just relax and wait here. I will be back with your passport in a few hours."

"Can I come with you?" I asked. But Amin didn't think that was a good idea.

"Let me deal with these guys. It's better this way," he replied.

After he left, I settled by the window for a long and anxious wait. I opened a new pack of Marlboro Lights and returned to my favorite occupation: people watching.

It normally took my minds off my worries, but today, my thoughts were elsewhere. In my mind, I was following Amin on the long drive to Murat's office. By my calculations, if the plan ran smoothly, he should be back in no more than three hours. And if all went according to plan, I would soon have access to a new life, free of abuse and fear.

I desperately needed that visa. When I was a teenager, I had at times rebelled against my family, especially my strict parents. But the trauma of my abusive marriage had highlighted the value of having my loved ones around me who had my back. I needed them in my life.

After the frustration of not being able to see them at Roya's wedding, I tried to imagine a festive reunion and thought of all the things I wanted to tell my big sister—the good moments, but also the heartaches and struggles too. And I wanted to hear about her own life as a newlywed in the US. Meanwhile, my parents were still sitting in Tehran, no doubt worried about their youngest daughter stranded in Istanbul. I hoped that they, too, would go to California soon so the entire family could gather for the first time in well over a decade.

Three hours passed, then five, then eight. I kept checking my watch. The sun went down and night rolled in. I had not left my spot by the window since Amin left that morning. I was still sitting there smoking, anxiously watching incoming traffic to the hotel in the hope of spotting his familiar silhouette as he walked in.

Sometime in mid-evening, it finally dawned on me that Amin would not come back. When the thought came to my head, I felt its impact physically—like a punch in the plexus that left me unable to breathe. I struggle to my feet but felt dizzy. The ground was swaying under my feet. I collapsed on the bed, overcome by the horror of what was happening. NO! My entire body was screaming. This could not be happening. NO!

It had all been a hoax, a scam! "Sweet" Amin had actually plotted from the start to defraud me of thousands of dollars. I had not eaten since breakfast, but my stomach churned. I felt sick and rushed to the bathroom.

Taking deep breaths, I tried to convince myself I was wrong. Amin WOULD come back, he WOULD call. He had promised. He'd be here any minute.

But while I tried hard to hold on to my faith that everything would turn out fine, the sinking feeling was growing. Deep down, I knew there was only one rational explanation: Amin was a crook who had exploited my vulnerable situation.

The night turned into morning and the sun came up. I had not slept a wink. Still no news of Amin nearly 24 hours after he had promised to return within a short period. By then, there was very little doubt left in my mind. Amin had betrayed me; he had conned me. That he had done so after hearing my story and knowing how much the visa meant for me was doubly painful.

Lying in bed, staring at the ceiling, I tried to make sense of it all. I had to get up and go to the call center. Roya would be waiting to hear the good news that I would soon be on my way, equipped with a new visa to Mexico.

Instead, I would have to admit that her and Rick's hard-earned money and my passport were gone. I wanted the earth to swallow me up. Better to be dead than to have to tell Roya what happened. Her little sister had screwed up again. I was ashamed and angry at myself for causing this catastrophe. A feeling of exhaustion washed over me. It felt like my life was an endless series of hurdles, betrayals and painful setbacks. I was tired to the bone of having to fight every day just to survive. Would life ever get easier?

My mind was buzzing and alert, but when I tried to get up, my body was frozen stiff. My legs would not respond. As a matter of fact, I could not lift a finger either. The link between my brain and my limbs had broken down. My muscles refused to respond. Something was wrong! Nothing moved. I tried again and again... nothing. The only thing I could move was my eyes. When I tried to make a sound, nothing came out.

What was happening to me? "GET UP" my mind was shouting. But it was hopeless.

I knew Roya would be worried if she didn't hear from me. I did not want her to think I had gone missing. I HAD to call her, now, and let her know that my plan to leave Istanbul had failed. I was still here, but the money had vanished. I stopped struggling as all my attempts to get up and move failed. "Someone will find me," I thought. Too distraught to even shed a tear, I closed my eyes. "This is it", I thought to myself. Stranded in Istanbul forever, paralyzed, all alone, with no friends, no family, no money, and no passport. I had hit rock bottom.

For a few hours, I just laid there, motionless, staring at the ceiling. Gradually, I felt pins and needles in my fingers and toes, then I was able to move my arms and finally my legs. As soon as I felt like I could stand, I got up. It was too soon. My body was not ready yet. The whole room started spinning, everything went dark and I fell back on the bed. I had not eaten since breakfast the day before. And I had spent 24 hours smoking and staring into space.

A few minutes later, I made another attempt, slower this time. What had happened to my brain and body? Could shock have caused an intense panic attack? Whatever the reason for my sudden paralysis, I did not have time to worry about it.

My priority was to call Roya. By then, it was the middle of the night in California and she must be beside herself with worry.

·   ·   ·

In the days before cheap communication over the Internet, long distance calls were expensive. Rather than using the costly hotel phone, at a premium, I always walked down the street to a call center where I could call long distance at a much cheaper rate.

I splashed cold water on my face and left my room. My tentative steps across the lobby were still a bit wobbly. I was not fully recovered yet and still felt like a zombie.

As I was exiting the hotel, I heard one of the front desk girls call my name. "Miss Naz…. Someone left something here for you," she yelled from behind the desk. Confused, I turned around and walked back towards her. "For me?" I asked.

She nodded and said, "Yes, there's an envelope for you", handing it to me. I tore it up with shaking hands and nearly collapsed. "OH MY GOD"! My passport! My passport… in the envelope! I nearly ripped it as I quickly leafed through its pages, hoping to find the Mexican visa I had been promised. But no stamp had been added since I had entrusted my travel document to Amin. He had taken the money, perhaps sharing the spoils with the Turkish man who was meant to provide the visa, but he had returned my passport. Surprising, for a man whose business was swindling travelers in need. It confirmed to me that an Iranian passport held little value, even to a professional crook.

"Is everything alright?" The front desk lady asked with concern when I turned deathly pale." Yes, Yes!" I replied.

But nothing was alright. "When was this envelope delivered? Who brought it? Did they leave another envelope perhaps?" I asked.

The young woman shook her head with a look of regret. She could see that I was in deep trouble.

"No, Ms. Naz. I am sorry, that is all we have. I don't know who brought it. I found the envelope on the counter."

"Are you sure? Please, can you take another look."

"Yes, I am certain, Ms. Naz," she replied sadly.

"Can you ask the others, please? Your co-workers. Please, it's very important."

She hesitated but saw what state I was in and said, "Sure, I will ask."

She disappeared into the back office but returned empty handed a few minutes later.

"I am sorry. I even called my colleague who was here for the night shift. There is nothing else. Can I help you with anything?", She asked again.

The defeated look on my face told her more than my few polite words. " No, nothing else. Thank you." I was devastated.

For an instant—a millisecond—when I saw the envelope, I thought that Amin had delivered on his promise or he had returned the money as well as the passport. Maybe he had had a last-minute change of heart and had decided not to go through with the illegal transaction, leaving money and passport at the hotel front desk before returning to Ankara.

But that was not the case. Amin had well and truly betrayed my trust. My only consolation, and it was not much, was that I still had my passport. Without a travel document, my situation would have been hopeless. Applying for a passport at the Iranian consulate would have led the authorities to question my situation and reach out to Hamid. By now, Hamid's authorization enabling me to travel outside Iran was long expired. At least, I had avoided this disaster. But now, I had to tell my sister about the other catastrophe—the theft of her savings. It was a cold fall morning and I felt the brisk cold air on my cheeks as I slowly walked through the streets of Istanbul. My gaze was fixed on the ground. When I stepped on the leaves, the crunch under my feet reminded me of a simpler time when I walked to our neighborhood bakery early morning to get fresh baked bread for breakfast.—a happy moment when I felt proud that my parents trusted me with this simple task and let me contribute to their duties.

As I approached the call center, I was still wondering how I would deliver the awful news to my sister and her new husband. I felt extremely guilty for losing the money.

I paid for the calling card and got into a private booth. After I dialed the long number, I heard my sister's voice after just one ring.

"Oh my God, Naz, what took you so long?! What happened, did you get it?"

The minute I heard Roya's voice, the floodgates opened. I had not shed a tear so far, but now they were running freely. Roya's voice had brought it home: This was real.

"What happened? What is going on Naz?" Roya asked nervously. "Say something. You're scaring me".

I finally managed to tell her what had happened.

"He never came back. Amin took the money and never came back," I cried. "I am so sorry, it's my fault. I am so sorry."

"What? What do you mean? Naz, are you ok? Did he hurt you?"

I cried even harder. It took a while until I was able to give Roya a full account of the past 24 hours—having breakfast with Amin, handing over the money and my passport, and the long wait through the night. I left out the fact that the shock had temporarily paralyzed me and that I was sick.

It broke my heart that after I had lost most of her savings, my sister was still worried asking if I was OK! Her strength amazed me. As always, she prioritized my wellbeing. With a shaky voice. I answered," Yes I'm alright, he didn't do anything to me. He left my passport at the front desk, but he took the money and disappeared."

"Ok, Ok... Are you sure he is really gone? Are you certain he is not coming back?" Roya asked.

I wanted to believe he would. I wanted to tell her there was still a chance that Amin would come back, but I could not lie to her. I knew that I had been scammed and I did not want to give Roya any false hope.

I hung up with a heavy heart, my eyes red and swollen. My head was pounding and I felt utterly deflated as I slowly walked back to the hotel.

Back to square one! We had to come up with a new plan and once again, it meant that I had to get into waiting mode—my life suspended as if in hibernation.

·   ·   ·

Time passed... I was so depressed that I lost count of the days. In my hotel room day and night, I lit up one cigarette after another, inhaling despair. I barely ate or slept. I was worn out and felt numb. Every day, for weeks, I dialed Amin's number, but it had been disconnected. The man had vanished.

With nothing to do, no plan to pin my hopes on, negative thoughts ran riot in my mind. An old familiar reel was running in a loop. Once again, I blamed myself. I second-guessed every decision, every move I'd made in my life. Maybe if I had listened to my dad from the start and had not t married Hamid, maybe if I had stayed in Tehran and lived a quiet life and never said anything to anyone, maybe if I had not given Amin all the money, maybe if I had done this or that...

Going out into the sunshine might have cleared my head and helped me gain some perspective. But I was too engulfed in self-pity, convinced that I had been dealt a bad hand in life. I could see no explanation for my setbacks. No rescue plan would ever succeed, I thought.

At this point, I was not Naz the rebel. Doubt and fear had carved a home for themselves in my brain. I was a naïve young woman who had trusted men undeserving of my confidence and was suffering the terrible consequences of my mistakes.

But it was time to let go and flush out negative, self-fulfilling beliefs out of my mind. Blaming myself served no purpose except holding me back. I had come too far to give up now, and quitting was not an option. Besides the consequences for myself, I owed it to my loved ones—Roya, Rick and my parents— to keep going. I could not let them down!

"Be strong, Naz! Keep up the fight!" I repeated, to kick myself out of my lethargy. I had spent enough time processing this latest blow. Now I had to pick myself up from the floor and fight the next battle.

CHAPTER ELEVEN

THE PROSPECTIVE MISTRESS

"If you expect respect from others, show it first to yourself. You cannot expect from others what you do not give to yourself."
–Shams Tabrizi

A few weeks later, I got word through my parents that a few of my friends from Tehran were coming to Istanbul on vacation. We had partied together and spent weekends at ski resorts—happy events that now belonged to a distant, more peaceful past.

That was great news! Just what I needed to distract me from my life in the waiting room. After spending so long on my own, I could use some company. I was craving human interaction and familiar faces. My exchanges with human beings in recent weeks had been limited to arguing with Tarik and demanding that he stop letting himself into my room and running away from male predators targeting me at the hotel.

To ensure we could spend as much time as possible together, my friends decided to stay in my hotel. I hadn't been in touch with any of them since I left Tehran. My mom, who had heard they were on their way to Istanbul, had reached out to them. I was careful to keep the conversation upbeat and avoided complaining too much on my weekly calls to my parents, but Mom knew I felt lonely. She thought it would do me good to see old friends.

Before telling them how to get in touch with me, she had made them promise to be discreet about my whereabouts and keep my location secret so Hamid would not find out. She knew they were close and loyal friends of mine, but my circles and Hamid's overlapped.

I ran down to the lobby when reception called to say that my four friends had arrived. We hugged and embraced each other for a while. Two of them had gotten married, the other two were still dating. It was an emotional moment, a reminder of times when good moments outweighed the bad, even if life in Tehran was often tough. In the last year of my marriage, locked up in Parvin's apartment, I had lost touch with my buddies and they did not know much of what had happened to me.

Once they settled into their rooms, we walked out to a nearby restaurant and had a festive meal. Then we returned to the hotel and continued talking all night. We had a lot of catching up to do!

For the rest of their stay, I pretended to be a tourist like them. I pushed aside thoughts of visas and dead ends to enjoy what Istanbul had to offer. After the debacle with Amin, I had mostly retreated to my hotel room and only left the hotel to get necessities or call my family. I was grateful for a semblance of normality and an opportunity to enjoy life with some of my closest friends.

We hit all the tourist venues. This time, I was able to guide them and relay information that Amin the Crook had given me on a previous visit. We saw Sultanahmet and admired its splendid turquoise tiles. We climbed to the gallery of Haghia Sofya, built as a church 1,500 years ago and later used as a mosque. The stone under our feet had been worn smooth by the countless worshippers, pilgrims and visitors who had walking on this ramp over centuries. The Sultan even rode his horse to reach the upper floor. From high up, the architectural splendor of the building evoked spiritual feelings even among non-believers.

I had briefly seen the Grand Bazaar with Amin, but was happy to explore its crowded alleys once more with my friends. We also strolled through the Spice Bazaar by the Golden Horn, breathing in smells that reminded me of home.

At night time, we tried a variety of restaurants—we had grilled fish one evening, Italian food the next and also sampled Turkish kebabs by the Golden Horn. We usually ended the evening in a bar perched high above the city. Istanbul had several rooftop venues that offering stunning views over the twinkling lights of the city at night. During the day, we hopped on the ferries that crisscrossed between the European and Asian shores. We even went all the way to the Black Sea on one of them, admiring the splendid wooden waterside mansions that lined the water on both sides.

My friends had heard that I'd left Hamid and was having a tough time. But they didn't know the extent of his abuse, nor the way his mother had treated me. They were horrified to hear the details and did their best to pamper me for a few days and help me forget my problems, even if only for a moment. I appreciated their efforts to make these few days as enjoyable as possible for me and tried not cloud their vacation by talking at length about my current predicament.

Arash, one of the four visitors, knew a prominent Iranian called Majeed, a family friend who had been living in Istanbul for a long time. On the last day of my friends' visit, Majeed pick us up from the hotel to show us his favorite places in the city.

After a leisurely breakfast, we all gathered in the lobby and chatted amicably while waiting to be picked up. We wanted to make the most of our time together. It was close to noon when Majeed showed up in his flashy car, a black, latest model BMW.

Majeed was a handsome, tall and fit man in his mid to late-40s who had left Iran after the revolution. Like many others who had fled the country, he ended up staying in Turkey, unable to travel further. He had made Istanbul his home and had done well for himself. Arash had told us that he had become a wealthy and powerful businessman, well known in the city. A few years earlier, he'd married a Turkish woman and now had a couple of kids.

After brief introductions, the five of us all squeezed in Majeed's car. He took us around town and showed us the more glamorous aspects of the city. His car, his clothes showed a man who was wealthy and enjoyed showing it. Iran and Turkey share a rich tradition of hospitality and Majeed wanted to welcome Arash and his travel companions to his adopted city in style. He took us to an expensive restaurant with a rooftop terrace overlooking the water and told us fascinating stories about his life in Istanbul.

While we were all chatting happily, Arash mentioned that I have been temporarily living in Istanbul while waiting to join my family in California. He proceeded to tell his friend how my money got stolen by an Iranian man who had promised to get me a visa on the black market. Majeed listened carefully to the story and expressed his sympathy.

"What is that man's name?" he asked.

"Amin", I said. "His name is Amin. He lives in Ankara but came here to meet me and supposedly arrange for the visa."

Majeed looked me straight in the eye and said,

"I know exactly who Amin is. I will get your money back, don't worry." I'd never expected to get the stolen money back. "You can't be serious. Are you sure it's the same guy?" I asked with hesitation.

Majeed replied confidently, "Yes, I am 100% sure. I know who he is. I will find this bastard and get your money back."

Surprise turned into joy and enormous relief. I had felt so guilty about losing Roya and Rick's money! "THANK YOU, THANK YOU SO MUCH," I said, trying to convey the immense gratitude I felt.

Maybe there were some good people left in this world willing to help others with no expectations of a reward, I thought. Majeed's offer, a random act of kindness, could perhaps restore my faith in fellow human beings, badly dented in recent months.

. . .

A couple of days after my friends headed back to Iran, the phone rang in my hotel room. I expected to hear Roya or my mom, but when I picked up, a man was on the line. "Naz?" I was a little confused. That wasn't my dad's or Rick's voice. " It's Majeed."

He had promised to contact me to discuss how he would get my money back, but I hadn't expected him to contact me so soon.

We spoke briefly and planned to meet the next day. He confirmed that one of his friends knew Amin personally and could track him down. We would meet this man and, with his help, force Amin to reimburse the stolen money.

The next day, I woke up happy that a solution to my money troubles was in sight. It would still not get me a visa to the US, but at the least I could let go of the heavy burden of guilt I'd been carrying since I was scammed.

Majeed was already in the lobby when I went down, holding court surrounded by Tarik and a few members of the hotel staff who seem to know who he was.

He excused himself and left the group when he saw me, and greeted me with a warm hug. As we stepped outside, I could feel the curious eyes of the hotel staff following us. Tarik looked especially surprised when I walked out with Majeed. He nodded a curt goodbye without saying a word.

Majeed and I got into his fancy car that he had parked right in front of the entrance, blocking access, and drove away followed by puzzled glances. Was Majeed such a well-known figure in Istanbul?

Dressed casually, his elbow resting confidently on the rolled-down window as he drove, Majeed peppered me with questions about my situation. Why did I want to go to America? Why couldn't I go back home? Why this and why that? After he finished interrogating me, it was my turn to ask questions. My mind was only focused on one thing: "Can you really get this thief to pay me back?"

His answer was," Yes, I will destroy this charlatan. Don't you worry."

We kept on driving. The avenue merged with the heavy traffic on the highway, leading us to the suspended bridge across the Bosphorus, an elegant feat of engineering spanning two continents and an architectural landmark of the city. After a while, we left the highway, driving through less affluent suburbs before entering a more rural zone. We were leaving the city behind. How weird!

"Um... Where are we going? Where does your friend live?" I asked, suddenly feeling uncomfortable.

"We are going on a road trip," Majeed calmly responded.

I was confused, "Why? Does your friend live far?"

"Oh, we are not going to see him today," Majeed said casually without looking my way.

"What do you mean? I don't understand. Where are you taking me exactly?"

This time, Majeed looked at me with a grin on his face:" It's a surprise."

I was getting very uncomfortable and slightly worried. My confidence knocked back by recent setbacks, I was no longer sure of my ability to judge character. Was Majeed a good guy or a threat? Circumstances had taught me that even if I thought I could look after myself, in countries like Iran and Turkey where men ruled supreme, I was still a vulnerable 23-years-old. Here, I was alone on unfamiliar territory with no one to help me. There were no cell phones at the time, and no one knew where I was or who I was with.

My reaction was colored by tough recent experiences—Amin's betrayal, Hamid's monstrous behavior, and Tarik, who was asked by my dad to look after me, but pursued other plans—but also an incident that had marked my early teens, one I had never revealed to anybody.------

I had barely reached puberty when a trusted friend of my father's touched me inappropriately during a visit to our home, seizing an opportunity when my parents were not present in the room.

He was a wealthy businessman who had given my dad work at a time when he needed it, allowing him to run his finances. My parents respected and trusted him. But over the following months, the man groped me several more times despite my best attempts to avoid being alone with him. My father would have murdered him if he'd ever found out.

When you are a young girl—still a child, really—forced by a family friend to endure intimate touches, you shut down and dissociate. I barely understood what was happening, but I was also acutely aware that it was wrong. I was in shock, frightened of the chain reaction that I would trigger if I spoke out. My old fashioned and strict upbringing at home combined with living under a government that denied women any rights had taught me to shut up and bury my pain.

So, afraid and ashamed, I kept silent like countless girls around the world subjected to sexual abuse. The few who do speak out are not always believed, especially if they live in traditional or religious societies.

I never said a word about it, although the man's unwelcome attentions hurt me and made me feel disgusted with myself. Now I know he was a pedophile, a criminal who used his power to molest a vulnerable young girl, knowing he enjoyed broad immunity. But at the time, I was overwhelmed by guilt and shame.

Years later, while advocating for abuse victims and survivors in the US, I would learn that victim blaming is not limited to Iran; it exists everywhere. As a result, all over the world, adults like me still carry the guilt and shame for most of their lives.

To distract myself, I focused on creative activities that allowed me to release my pent-up emotions. All those artistic forms, from poetry writing to painting and drawing helped me cope with those traumatic incidents. My parents never suspected a thing. But the panic I experienced each time the man approached me and the shame that washed over me kept me in a dark place for a very long time and part of me died.

In the following years, as I grappled with the memories and the trauma of these events, I resolved that I would never again be a silent victim. I thought I could avoid further trauma.

But I learned the hard way that no matter how old you are or your location in the world, being a woman often came at a price and risks were everywhere. I had to remain on the alert and build a wall around myself. It was never safe to let my guard down. To survive in a male-dominated world filled with misogyny and avoid being targeted repeatedly, you had to develop street smarts. I had to take control and fight back.

.   .   .

Sitting next to Majeed in the car, I was getting danger signals. My palms were clammy as these memories of indecent assaults came flooding back. Paranoia was setting in quickly. "Where are you taking me?" I asked Majeed again more firmly.

He replied, "Relax... sit back and get comfortable. We still have another hour to go."

An hour! I sunk into my seat, now seriously worried that I had put myself in a tricky situation. There was nothing I could do now but wait to find out. Had I put my trust in the hands of a stranger too quickly, AGAIN? My desperate situation forced me to pin my hopes on these guys and I hated having to take these risks for fear of missing a crucial opportunity. Tense, I reminded myself that Majeed was not a random guy. My old friend Arash who had introduced us had known him for years. After driving past fields and through woods for what felt like forever, we finally arrived at our destination - a small resort by the Black Sea.

I was feeling unsteady on my feet as I followed Majeed down a steep stairway to reach a beautiful cliffside villa. He already had a key in his hand and opened one of the doors and told me to get inside ahead. I stepped into a large, airy room, dominated by a king-size bed. I stood next to it, not knowing what to do or say. My worst fears were justified as Majeed's intentions became clear. But I would not give in. My gut was telling me to stand my ground and not show weakness. I would not cry or beg. I sensed that I stood a better chance if I acted confident and strong. Majeed was not the kind of a man who would respond well to tears or desperation, I knew that much.

I casually asked him what we were doing here and how long we'd stay.

"Just the night," he said with a smile, "We'll have some fun tonight and we'll go back to the city tomorrow."

"I won't stay here. I want to go back to the city immediately," I said.

"Why are you in such a hurry, honey? We'll have a good time."

Honey? When did we get so comfortable with each other? "I want to go back to the hotel," I repeated, trying to sound a lot more confident than I felt.

"Think, Naz! Think. Quickly!" I told myself. "Whatever you do, don't cry".

I had to dig deep into my reserves of mental strength to deal with this hazardous situation. The successive blows I'd experienced in recent months had drained me emotionally. But they had also made me tougher. I was tough as nails by now—or so I wanted to believe—and I had to show it.

While I still stood awkwardly by the bed, unwilling to sit down, Majeed stretched out on the other side. He tapped the bed with his hand, inviting me to lay next to him. His intentions could not be clearer. I had fallen into another trap but this time I would get out. I was angry and sick and tired of being taken advantage of by these men, I was determined to turn this situation around. Internally, I kicked myself for being so naive. To think that I'd believed Majeed was a nice man who'd volunteered selflessly to help me. I should have known that he would want something in return.

Majeed had seen a young woman alone, desperate to reunite with her family and in need of help, and like Amin, he'd decided to take advantage of the situation. Except that he did not want money. He wanted me.

Another name to add to my list of ruthless predators! I now realized that the interrogation in the car was designed to learn about my vulnerabilities so he could exploit them more easily. He wanted to make sure that no one in Istanbul was looking after me.

I had cleared significant hurdles in my life, and I would get over this one too. But I had to act quickly.

"You don't really know Amin, do you?" I asked." You can't get my money back. This was just a hook to get me here." He looked at me, surprised. He had not expected me to confront him head on. Deep down, I was petrified.

"I'll give you seven thousand dollars. Hell, I'll give you ten thousand, honey. Don't worry!" he said. "Stay here with me, stay in Istanbul. I can get you your own house and you won't even have to work. I can take care of you and give you everything you need."

Whoa! Majeed had my future all mapped out. I couldn't believe what I was hearing: He was propositioning me and wanted me to become a paid mistress.

His offer was so outrageous that I yelled at him. "No way! Absolutely not. I intend to leave and join with my family. Plus, you have a wife and kids."

He looked at me, raised an eyebrow and said in a matter-of-fact voice:" SO?"

I was getting really angry. No way would I give in to his demands. Then I remembered that the entire hotel staff had watched us leave together. Here was a card I could play. Maybe it would work.

"Listen Majeed, you are a well-known guy in this city. I know you have a reputation to protect. Tarik, who works at the hotel's front desk, is a friend of my dad's and he is keeping an eye on me. He knows I am with you right now. He has seen us leave together and I also told him early this morning that we were attending a meeting together and would be back in a couple of hours. He knows you and he has your license plate number."

I could see that Majeed was getting uneasy. This was not going according to plan. He had expected me to submit meekly.

Before, I could continue, he shouted,"Damn it! Why did you do that?"

His evident discomfort suggested that my strategy was working. He believed me.

"Why?" I continued, "Because you are a stranger and I am in a foreign country. I didn't know you well enough to trust you—and it turns out I was right. You lied to get me here and you exploited the fact that I'm alone. Shame on you! You are no better than Amin. Did you seriously believe I would agree to have an affair with a total stranger."

I could see that Majeed was making calculations in his head. In the end, he apparently concluded that it was not worth the potential trouble. Getting off the bed, he grabbed his car keys, looking furious. "Let's go."

I was bitterly disappointed that the alleged mission to get my money back had turned into an attempt to get me into bed. But I was also very relieved to have escaped so lightly, and proud to have stood my ground.

The ride back to the hotel was uncomfortably quiet. A wall had descended between us and we didn't exchange a word until we reached the city. Just before we arrived at the hotel, Majeed tried to convince me one last time to stay in Istanbul. "You could have an apartment, money for as much shopping as you want and a good life in Istanbul," he said. "I'd even give you money to repay your sister." In addition to looking after me, he would help me get Turkish citizenship. Then I would easily get a visa to visit my family in California, he claimed.

Majeed was barking up the wrong tree. Much as I wanted to reimburse Roya and Rick, I could not even consider accepting his offer. This was dirty money and I wasn't that kind of girl.

Now that I was on safer ground, my earlier fear was replaced with full-blown fury. How did this man, twice my age, with a family of his own, have the audacity to ask me point blank to be his mistress. He'd probably never heard the word "No."

I didn't bother saying a word. I kept my eyes firmly focused on the cityscape scrolling outside the car window. No point provoking him and getting into a confrontation that could get me harmed. He was a jerk! End of story. Another lesson learned! Once again, my trust had been misplaced.

When he slowed down in front of the hotel, I jumped out before the car had even come to a full stop. He grabbed my arm before I was out of reach and said, "Call me if you change your mind, you have my number."

And as I was stepping into the lobby, he rolled down his window and yelled, "Wait." I looked over my shoulder. "Could you please not mention what happened today to Arash? They are family friends. They don't need to know." I shook my head, even more disgusted, and ran inside the hotel. "Pathetic loser!" I thought.

Once inside my room, I locked the door behind me and sat on the floor. That's when the tension of the past few hours hit me. I began to shake uncontrollably and burst into tears. I would not get Roya's money back. Another huge disappointment, but I knew that in the circumstances, I had also been lucky. Out there, Majeed could have raped me and locked me up. Why was this happening to me over and over again? Did I have a big target on my back or was there a sign on forehead saying "PREDATORS AND CREEPS WELCOME"?

I could not wrap my mind around the succession of horrible events I was experiencing. When would this stop? I felt I was breaking into a million pieces. But I had to keep meltdowns behind closed doors and dig deep for strength, even if the tank felt empty. Today, I had managed to talk myself out of a tricky situation. This was no small achievement.

I did not tell Roya or my parents about that incident. There was no reason to add to their worries. I'd had a narrow escape. The situation with Majeed could have turned far worse. But I also felt that, after making the initial mistake of trusting him—not unreasonably due to his connection with Arash—I'd saved the day.

•   •   •

Weeks dragged on and my visitor's permit was about to expire. Although Iranians did not need a visa to enter Turkey, we could not stay for more than three months at a time. To avoid breaking the law, I would have to leave the country and re-enter, therefore getting the right to stay legally for another three months. With no visa to travel anywhere, how would I achieve that? Discussing it with my family, I initially suggested flying to Tehran or another Iranian city for a few hours before hopping on a return flight to Istanbul, but Roya and my parents categorically vetoed this proposal. We couldn't be sure if Hamid had reported my "disappearance" to the authorities and I ran the risk of being arrested the minute I touched Iran's soil. Besides, the written permission he'd given to leave Iran had expired. I might not be able to get out again. They were right, of course. It was a huge risk that I couldn't afford to take. But after three months in Istanbul, my judgment was clouded by homesickness.

After much debate, we decided I would fly to Cyprus—another place I could visit without a visa. I would fly in, stay for a few hours, and get on the next plane to Istanbul. Roya made all the arrangements from California and sent me the reservation details. The only flight we could find was a red-eye that would get me to Cyprus in the middle of the night. I'd return to Istanbul in the morning.

I had never been on an airplane before and I was excited to take to the skies, even on this short trip. This felt like a bit of an adventure, especially as I knew very little about the Mediterranean island of Cyprus. All I'd heard was that it was a popular vacation spot for Europeans, but I wouldn't get to enjoy its beaches. After a few short hours at the airport, I'd return to Istanbul.

As this was an evening flight, I did not get to enjoy much of the view apart from watching the glittery lights of Istanbul disappear below us as the plane gained altitude. The vast city seemed to spread over an enormous surface area.

After a short hop, we landed on the small island. After deplaning, I followed the crowd to the main area of the airport, which had few amenities and looked more like a hangar than an airport. There was no seating or rest area. The stores that sold food, drinks, and souvenirs were closed for the night.

Outside it was dark and we seemed to be in the middle of nowhere. I had expected a modern airport serving an upmarket tourist destination. My first impression of Cyprus was not at all what I had pictured.

I later learned that since 1974, the island was divided. The popular tourist paradise was in the more affluent Greek part of the island, in the south. My Turkish Airlines flight had touched down in the less developed northern enclave, which had close ties with Turkey and was occupied by Turkish troops.

The air was humid and hot in the airport, and cicadas were singing outside. A few people were slumped on the floor, trying to get some sleep. Maybe, like me, they were transients waiting for the next flight out. I found an empty corner and sat on the floor. I felt sleepy, but kept my eyes wide open and my mind alert. I felt too exposed to fall asleep. I kept my belongings close to my body to avoid getting robbed, and avoided making eye contact with people passing by.

Another unfamiliar place, another weird episode in my saga. My mood was on a constant roller coaster. Periods of hope were followed by crashing disappointments. At times, I felt capable of taking on the world to achieve my dreams of freedom and artistic endeavor. But these moments alternated with waves of despair and helplessness that threatened to engulf me when I felt I was making no progress toward my goal.

In this bleak airport, waiting for the flight to return to Istanbul—a city that at least offered a degree of familiarity—uncertainty was on my mind. Dissociating, almost as I was floating in the air, I could watch myself from above, sitting on that cold dirty floor, surrounded by middle-aged men fast asleep and snoring loudly. How had I got here? Did my mistakes lead to my current predicament? I couldn't remember a time when life was not fraught with difficulties.

More than once during brief moments of depression, I had contemplated going back to Iran and the devil who was waiting for me there. Thankfully, my common sense always gained the upper hand quickly. And when it didn't, I could always count on Roya to knock some sanity into me. I was growing wiser and shrewder by the day. Somehow, along a path strewn with disappointments and betrayals, I had picked up some street smarts. The way I successfully brushed off Majeed's advances showed that I'd successfully learned a few tricks. I had to keep my head clear and fight on.

In the morning, exhausted but relieved to get out of the barren airport, I boarded my flight to Istanbul and returned to the hotel. After a sleepless night, it almost felt like home. I crashed on my bed, grateful that I had made it back safely. I now had permission to stay another three months in Istanbul. But I had no intention to be here that long. I would be out way ahead of the next expiration date.

It was still early when I got back and I briefly considered freshening up and going downstairs for breakfast, but before I even had time to decide, I drifted off into a deep sleep.

CHAPTER TWELVE

AN UNEXPECTED BLESSING

"It is pointless trying to know where the way leads. Think only about your first step, the rest will come."
–Shams Tabrizi

One cold October evening, as I was warming up a can of Gormeh Sabzi—a delicious Persian stew of meat, beans and herbs—on a little portable electric stove that my mom, concerned that I was not eating enough, had somehow managed to send me from Iran, I got a call from Roya.

My sister had news for me, exciting news. She'd discussed my situation in Istanbul with Emma, one of her closest friends. The two of them had met in Tehran a few years earlier when Emma spent about a year there for work. Born in Panama, Emma had lived in several countries, including Spain. Roya used to take her out and show her around Tehran, and they would attend parties together. In no time, they became fast friends and remained in touch even after both of them left Iran.

I remembered Emma as a beautiful and kind young woman I had met a few times with my sister. She came from a diplomatic family, which is why Roya had contacted her to ask if she had suggestions on how I could get out of Turkey.

It turned out Emma did have an idea. Her father was the Ambassador of Panama in London. She reached out to him, told him the details of my story, stressing that I would be in danger if I returned to Iran, and asked if he could help. After days of brainstorming, they came up with a plan: He would grant me a visa to Panama.

Emma arranged for me to mail my passport to her dad in London. Panama was nowhere near California and I was hesitant at first. But then I reflected and realized that flying to the tiny nation would at least get me across the Atlantic and much closer to my final destination.

It was also a lot further from Iran and less accessible to Iranians. In Panama, I'd be even less likely to come across friends of Hamid. It would be a significant step forward. So, I gladly agreed to give this proposal a try. I had little to lose and much to gain if it worked. And I owed it to my loyal sister to go along with any plan she devised. I had to pursue all possibilities.

The next day, I went to the post office and mailed my passport to the Panamanian embassy in London. I was aware that this move wasn't without risk. Without my passport to prove my identity and the stamp to show when I'd entered Turkey, I could run into trouble with the local authorities. The passport could also get lost in transit. International mail, after all, was not always reliable. If that happened, I would be in the situation I had narrowly avoided, when I thought that Amin had stolen my passport as well as my money. I would have no way to replace a lost passport without getting involved with the dreaded Iranian authorities, something I wanted to avoid at all costs.

A couple of weeks went by, then one morning after my daily visit to the breakfast buffet, run, Tarik intercepted me as I was heading to my room. "Naz, You've got mail." He handed me a small but thick envelope with a flag on the cover that I assumed was Panamanian. I thanked him profusely and got into the elevator. Once on my floor, I rushed down the corridor to my room and ripped the envelope open. Inside was my passport, with a brief note from Emma's father, the Panama ambassador, that said:

"Dear Naz, I have provided you with a visa to Panama. This is the best I could do. I hope it helps. Good luck on your journey."

My heart was pounding with joy. It was a happy moment. Finally, a step forward and an opportunity to leave Turkey!

I knew nothing about Panama, beyond what I'd learned in my geography class in high school when we learned about the construction of the canal, but after being stranded in Istanbul for months, I'd have gone anywhere. I would soon be ON THE MOVE!

I rushed out of the hotel and ran towards the call center. I finally had positive news to deliver and I couldn't wait to tell Roya, who heard my downbeat voice all too often. This time, as soon as she picked up the phone, I screamed: "I got it,

Roya, I got it! I have a visa to Panama." After repeatedly hitting closed doors, I had my passport in my hand with a shiny new visa to a country much closer to the U.S.

I could hear the relief in my sister's voice, "THANK GOD! Finally, something."

. . .

But when Roya tried to plan my itinerary, a new issue emerged that we had not expected. "Naz, I've been looking for tickets and there's a problem," Roya told me during a call the next day. "There are no direct flights from Istanbul to Panama. You'll have to travel via Europe and to do that, you need a transit visa for the layover." When I cleared one hurdle, another appeared. Being an Iranian carried a heavy cost. Even for a brief layover between two flights at a European airport, I needed to obtain a transit visa.

"What a pain!" I moaned. "I will go to the German or maybe the Italian Consulate tomorrow and try my luck there." It would just be a formality, I thought, since I wouldn't even leave the airport. But I'd learned not to take anything for granted. I'd rejoice once I had a transit visa. "I'll keep you posted," I told my sister before we ended our conversation. No reason to panic, I told myself. This will easily be sorted.

The next morning, I was still in an upbeat mood at the prospect of leaving Istanbul and seeing my siblings. The transit issue was a minor setback, but I would soon deal with it.

After a quick shower, I chose my clothes carefully. I dressed more formally than I had in recent weeks and applied some makeup to make a good impression. Grabbing my passport, I headed out early. I was in a hurry to reach the German Consulate, near Istanbul's central Taksim square, on the other side of the Golden Horn. I was confident that within a couple of hours, I would be calling my sister again and telling her to book my ticket.

Many people were already assembled in a long line on the pavement when I got to the Consulate. Some had arrived before daybreak to get ahead. I took my place at the back of the queue and waited patiently. In the meantime, I filled out a couple of forms that an official was handing out to the people waiting. Having answered each question carefully, I placed the documents inside my passport, on the page where the all-important visa to Panama was stamped, ready to present them to the agent in charge. A couple of hours later, I was finally inside the Consulate. My turn has come to make my case to the consular official.

With a big smile on my face, I handed my passport along with the necessary forms to the middle-aged man on the other side of the glass partition who looked very German with his fair skin, brown hair and blue eyes sitting behind a desk.

He took my documents and gave me a weary look. Another visa applicant! He probably had a boring job, processed hundreds of visa requests every day. After asking me a few basic questions—why am I going to Panama? Why am I in Istanbul? Why did I want to travel via Germany? And some that I found somewhat intrusive and random—he told me to wait and disappeared into a back office. After a few long minutes, he returned with my passport in hand.

With question marks in my eyes, I looked at him, holding my breath. I tried to read his face, but it was inscrutable and I couldn't figure out if he'd accede to my request. He took his time sitting back in chair and adjusting the papers on his desk, before turning to me and handing me my passport.

"I'm sorry," he said before I grabbed the document. "We can't grant you a transit visa."

I looked at him bewildered, trying to process what he had just said. After the initial shock wore off, I asked, "Sir, can you tell me why? I just need to transit visa for a couple of hours while my flight stops in Frankfurt. I won't even leave the terminal. Please?"

Any hope that I could persuade him to give me the damn transit visa quickly proved unfounded. He just shook his head and said " I am sorry, you have to go back to your own country to apply for the visa. We have a German embassy in Tehran. You can try there."

Fighting tears, I managed to hold it together long enough to tell him that I couldn't go back to Iran. This was awful! I had escaped an abusive husband and going back would be risky. But nothing I said had an impact. Accustomed to crushing applicants' hopes, he expressed neither pity nor sympathy for my plight. "It is procedure," he said. "There is nothing I can do." The answer was "No."

I went back to the hotel feeling deflated. My buoyant mood has vanished. I sat on my bed and waited for Roya to call at a time we had arranged. When I told her what had happened, she said, " It's ok, don't be disappointed. That was just the first embassy! There are many other countries in Europe you can go through to get to Panama."

Sensing my flagging spirits, she remained upbeat throughout our conversation. "Try a different embassy tomorrow, one of them will give you a transit visa, I'm sure of it. The most important thing is that you have a visa to a destination. One of these countries will stamp a transit visa in your passport without thinking twice about it. Don't lose hope."

I wanted to believe her. For my own sanity, I needed to hold on to the hope of leaving Istanbul soon. It had been such months since I'd sought refuge here and I was more than ready to move on, especially after experiencing several major setbacks. My emotional reserves were running low and after each knock, it got a bit harder to bounce back and hold on to my optimism. But I had to!

The next morning, I rose early again and went through the same motions. I was on a mission, determined to achieve my goal. I made myself presentable, this time for the Italians. If I had no success at their Consulate, I would move on to the U.K consulate and then to the French representation.

Day after day, I ran all over town, rushing from one European consulate to the next to plead my case. I spent a lot of time staring at flags of various colors and standing in line among people who harbored similar hopes and doubts, ahead of their moment of reckoning in front of the consular officers. Most of the other visa applicants were Turks, and they too, faced obstacles when traveling abroad. But I also heard quite a few of my compatriots speaking Farsi in the lines, though I avoided engaging with them.

Every single consulate I applied to turned me down and refused to issue a transit visa. The answer was the same everywhere. "We have an embassy in Tehran. You need to go back to your own country to apply for a visa."

Did these countries not understand Iran's political environment? Did they not grasp that going back was not an option for me? "It is the policy", was the standard answer.

My objective—leaving Istanbul—was almost within reach, but bridging the last gap was proving tough. Was the world conspiring to keep me apart from my family? I had nearly exhausted legal means. But when I tried illegal ones, I got badly burned. Was it a sign? Should I just go back to Iran? Every time another rejection made me want to give up, Roya reminded me of what was at stake. "We've come too far to abandon now," she'd say. "Hang on another day. It will work out. I know it."

Tired, hopeless, disappointed, and afraid, I was running out of options. Walls were closing in on me, shutting out the light and hope of a new life. I was trapped in Istanbul, this hotel, this room. My mood was again spiraling down, my mind jumping from one paranoid thought to another. Would I be stuck here forever, unable to take a step back or moving forward?

I had arrived in Istanbul in high summer when the hot and humid air made my clothes cling to my body. It was now fall and trees were shedding their leaves. I even had to buy a couple of sweaters to keep warm when I left the hotel. How many more seasonal changes would I witness in this city? I'd never expected to stay here so long.

My sister, as usual, provided unconditional support. Without her support and her determination, I would never have survived through these long months. Roya and I were talking on the phone every day, trying to come up with new scenarios. The rest of the time, when I wasn't watching passers-by from my bedroom window, I was doodling in a sketch book I had bought to keep myself busy... and sane.

· · ·

And then, an unexpected encounter turned the tide just as winter was approaching. One dark and freezing night in November, after another frustrating attempt at getting a transit visa, I walked back to my hotel feeling despondent.

It had been a long day but I decided to walk instead of hailing a cab. I needed to stretch my legs and clear my head, as well as save money. I dreaded the thoughts that crept into my head during those lonely nights when I was cooped up in my small hotel room. Losing myself in the dense crowd that permanently filled Istanbul's streets gave me a sense of normality. I am a city girl at heart and love the hustle and bustle of a big metropolis. That night, while the cold air felt as sharp as a knife against my skin, it made me feel alive.

When I reached the hotel, instead of heading straight to my empty room, as I normally did, I decided to sit in the lobby for a few minutes and warm up with a cup of tea.

The hotel was unusually animated that night. A group of tourists had just arrived and were standing by the desk with their suitcases, visibly excited about their visit to the former Ottoman capital.

People watching took my mind away from another disappointing day, marked by more rejections. Different groups of people were sitting around the small tables in the lobby, chatting and laughing loudly while enjoying the sugar hit of Turkish baklava, a sticky and sweet dessert composed of thin pastry layers, honey and pistachio nuts. As I sipped my tea, re-running the latest encounters with consulate officials in my mind, I noticed that a young lady sitting at a nearby table was trying to get my attention. "Hello! What's your name?" I smiled and said, "Hi, I am Naz."

With a pleasant smile, she asked me in Farsi, " Are you Iranian?" I responded in the language of my birth, "Yes I am."

She lit up, "Nice to meet you, Naz. I'm Shirin. We're all visiting from Tehran, except Sina." She pointed to one of the men—a tall dark-haired man in his late thirties who hadn't shaved in a few days. "He is from Holland... I mean he's Iranian but he lives in Holland. We'd all arranged to meet here in Istanbul and we spent a few days here. We're all going back to Tehran tomorrow, except Sina of course. He was supposed to go back to Amsterdam, but he lost his passport. He has to get a temporary one before he can fly back home," she explained. "I mean, who loses their passport?! Only him!" The entire group erupted in laughter while Sina made a funny face, looking sheepish. He then joined in and laughed as his friends teased him.

"What about you Naz? How long are you staying in Istanbul?" Shirin asked.

I gave Shirin and her friends an edited version of my story. I didn't provide details but said I couldn't go back to Iran and had been stuck in Istanbul for several months on my way to Panama, because I was unable to get a transit visa.

They were intrigued and invited me to their table. In spite of my wariness toward fellow Iranians, I decided to join them and was introduced to the rest of the group. We ordered drinks and continued our conversation. They were a nice group, cheerful and welcoming. I needed friendly human interactions after my grueling days queuing at consulates and it felt good to speak my native language. An evening with fellow humans provided a welcome change from the lonely nights in my room. If nothing else, it would distract me from my problems for a few hours.

At the end of the evening as we were parting ways and saying our goodbyes, Sina turned to me and said, "I have to go to the Dutch consulate tomorrow morning to apply for a temporary passport so I can get back home. Why don't you come with me? I speak Dutch and can try to convince the consulate to give you a transit visa." I explained that it would be pointless because I'd already been to that consulate where Dutch consular officers had flatly turned me down. "Why not give it a try anyway?" said Sina. "It sounds like you have nothing to lose. Let me help, you never know." Then he continued with a cheeky smile, "I have persuasion skills like no other."

A man offering his help? I'd been down that road before and fallen into the trap. This made me hesitant. But after briefly reflecting on Sina's offer, I realized that he was right: I had nothing to lose. Going to the Dutch consulate in broad daylight would not be too risky. We'd be in a public place the entire time and I could leave whenever I wanted to.

So, I agreed. It was worth a try, even if it ended up bringing more grief. Having another go at obtaining this elusive transit visa was better than wasting another day ruminating about my fate in that hotel room.

.   .   .

In the morning, Sina and I met in the lobby. We hailed a cab in front of the hotel and headed to the Consulate of the Netherlands, on Istiklal Street, in the heart of the city. A mile-long pedestrian street, Istikal was perpetually filled with a dense crowd. The cab dropped us in Tunel, by the tramway stop, and we struggled to walk against the tide of people flowing along the store-lined street.

Sina kept up small talk while we weaved between people, trying to advance toward our destination. We eventually reached the huge gate of the Dutch consulate, built during Ottoman times, when Istanbul, then called Constantinople, was the capital of the Ottoman empire. Istiklal (Independence) Street was then Pera, and it was the main hub for Europeans who settled in the Ottoman capital.

Encouraged by Sina's calm attitude, I tried to block out the negative chatter in my head. I'd confronted too many implacable consular officers in recent weeks to feel confident about this latest attempt. But Roya and I had determined that we would leave no stone unturned. By returning to the Dutch consulate with Sina, I was going the extra mile.

We had to wait for about thirty minutes before we could be seen by an agent. When the previous applicant left the office and Sina's turn came, he gestured, inviting me to go in with him.

Sina was speaking in fluent Dutch with the tall and skinny official, who appeared in his late thirties. I couldn't understand a word of what they were saying, but it sounded like the two men were joking and having a friendly conversation. I could tell that the agent was finding Sina entertaining. I assumed my compatriot was telling him a funny story about how he had lost his passport. Perhaps Sina was trying to be friendlier than usual since he had an additional request to submit after sorting out his own situation. Whatever he was saying, his charm was obviously working. The agent left the office and returned with a document that appeared to be Sina's temporary travel document.

They shook hands and exchanged some more words in Dutch. As they chatted, Sina pointed in my direction and they both turned to me. After a few minutes of back and forth, which sounded more serious than their earlier conversation, Sina asked for my passport. I handed it to the agent, giving him a nervous smile. He went to the back office again while we waited. By then, I was used to the sick feeling in the pit of my stomach—I felt like a defendant awaiting the official verdict at the end of a trial.

Curious, I asked Sina what he had told the Dutch official. He answered in a quiet voice, almost whispering as if the agent could understand Farsi, "I told him that you are my niece and you need a transit visa to make your way to Panama. I added that we hoped to fly together as far as Amsterdam. He initially said it was not possible, but I insisted and I think I've convinced him." Then he winked and continued, "Let's hope he comes back with a stamp in your passport."

I could feel hope rising within me, but I had to contain it. My heart was racing, my palms were sweaty, and I felt faint just thinking of the possibility that it could work.

The agent finally re-appeared from the back office, walked towards me and handed me my passport. "Safe travels, Miss," he said, with a twinkle in his eye.

I was stunned. "Thank you, THANK YOU!" I didn't want to look overly excited because it might have been suspicious. I couldn't believe Sina had managed to sweet talk the Dutch official. As we walked out of the embassy, I opened my passport. Magic! There it was... a transit visa to Holland stamped in my passport on the page following the one that contained my Panama visa. My eyes welled up with tears and I gave Sina a big hug outside the consulate. "You have no idea what you just did for me, I don't know how to thank you". He smiled and said, "I'm just happy I could help."

The cab ride back to the hotel was one of the most joyful moments I'd experienced in a very long time. My heart was exploding with gratitude and happiness. This time, it seemed that we had successfully overcome the last obstacle. I was in the last stretch and could race to the finish.

.   .   .

The minute we got back to the hotel, I rushed to the call center. My feet were barely touching the ground—I was flying. I did not care if it was 4:00 AM or 4:00 PM in California. I had to tell her ASAP. I was thrilled to have good news to report after weeks of burdening her with my problems.

The phone rang, once, twice and on the third ring I heard a man's raspy and sleepy voice from the other side of the line.

"...Hello?"

"Hi... Rick? It's me, Naz. I am so sorry to call you so late, hmm, or so early. Sorry! I haven't even checked what time it is there. Forgive me, but I need to speak to my sister right away."

"No worries, dear. Is everything ok?" he asked.

"Yes, everything is great, actually."

Rick handed the phone to Roya, who had woken up from her slumber. I could hear the concern in her voice. She was probably expecting another setback, especially at this unusual time.

"Roya," I said with voice shaking with excitement. "I've got it! I got a transit visa to Holland."

I could picture her sitting up in her bed, turning the light on. I heard her scream with glee, "Rick, Rick! She can leave Istanbul! She got the visa."

By the time I was done telling the story of my chance encounter with Sina in the hotel lobby and how he'd helped me get the transit visa to Holland, we were both screaming with joy. I could hear Rick in the background saying, "Congratulations, we did it!"

Roya promised she would make travel arrangements and buy a plane ticket right away so I wouldn't have to stay in Istanbul a minute longer than necessary. I would go to Panama and we would then figure the rest of my journey from there.

That night, I slept like a baby, finally at peace. I woke up late and strolled down for a leisurely breakfast, taking the time to enjoy my traditional Turkish breakfast of tea, feta cheese, fresh bread, honey, eggs, tomatoes, cucumber and olives. Now, I just needed to wait for my plane ticket. No more consulate runs, no more applications to fill out. I just had to wait for Roya's instructions.

She called me later that day.

"Listen carefully," she said, "We're changing the plan slightly. I've booked you a flight to Panama via Amsterdam."

This didn't sound like a change of plan. What was different? "You're going to have a 12-hour layover in Amsterdam. When you get off the plane in Amsterdam, stay in the transit area of the airport. There is a hotel where you can stay. Get a room for two nights for two people.

"But why?" I asked surprised. "I don't need a hotel Roya. I can just sleep in the airport or browse through the stores until it's time to board my flight to Panama. It's not a problem" I replied.

She interrupted me. "Look... I don't want you to go to Panama anymore." My sister went on to explain that once I reached Amsterdam, her husband Rick would join me. Although I could not leave the airport and go into the city, I could stay in the transit area as long as I wanted. Rick would bring our cousin Sahar's American passport with him. "You are going to pretend you are Sahar and travel with her passport."

"Sahar?" I said in disbelief. My cousin had settled in the US years earlier and she was at least a decade older than me. "She is a lot older than me and we don't look at all alike!" I said.

I could hear that Roya was getting a little impatient." Yes, I know. I suggest you go find a hair salon and get your hair dyed blond. Her hair is very light in her passport picture."

"Ok, but..." I was in shock. "No buts Naz, I need you to be brave," Roya said. "I don't have my US passport yet or I would send it to you, but we can't wait anymore. She looks more like you than I do anyway." Roya felt we had to seize this opportunity. I couldn't stay in Istanbul any longer and the detour via Panama would only create additional complications. Instead, from Amsterdam, Rick and I would board a flight to Mexico City with my cousin's US passport, thus eliminating the need for a visa. "We are doing this. It's the only way," Roya said, putting an end to the discussion.

"We've already tried everything else."

Traveling on my cousin's passport seemed risky and an extreme measure. But then, so much was at stake—my life, my future—and we had to be bold. I did not know my cousin Sahar well, but she was close to my older sisters who were of a similar age.

The next day I arranged for a hair appointment at a nearby salon I'd often walked past on my regular walks to the phone center. The place didn't look very fancy, but it was clean and decent.

"I would like to dye my hair blond," I told the hairstylist, a well-dressed guy in his late 20s. He looked at my dark brown hair and asked, "Are you sure? Not just a shade or two lighter? Maybe some lowlights?"

" Yes, I'm sure. I want to go the whole way. Blond please!" I showed him a picture of Sahar taken at Roya's wedding to illustrate the shade I wanted. He was hesitant and pointed out that going from dark brown to light blond in one sitting was a risky move. It's a process usually done gradually over several visits. "How about we do it in two sessions?" he asked.

I insisted that I would be leaving town soon and couldn't afford to delay. He nodded reluctantly before moving to the back of the salon where I saw him mixing colors in a plastic bowl.

He was taking his time to do the job properly, careful not to overexpose my hair to the aggressive chemicals that would strip it of its natural color before turning it blond. He checked that the dye was working its magic on several occasions before rinsing it out and washing my hair. We both crossed our fingers and hoped my hair wouldn't fall out once the job was done.

By the time I left the salon a few hours later, I was as blond as a Norwegian baby.

Roya wanted me to get out as soon as possible and she had booked me on the same flight as Sina. It was taking off the next evening. She thought Sina could help me settle at the airport in Amsterdam since he was a local and knew his way around. All economy tickets had sold out, and at short notice, the only seats available were in first class. I offered to take a different flight, maybe the following day, to reduce costs. But Roya felt traveling with Sina was the safest option and an opportunity we had to seize.

Everything was suddenly happening very fast. The next morning, I packed up anything worth taking with me and left the rest in the corner of my little hotel room for the maids to take home or trash.

I looked around the room. If these walls could talk, they'd have many tales to tell about the ups and downs—downs, mostly—I'd experienced in the past few months. Day after day, I'd sat by the window smoking countless packs of cigarettes, feeling homesick, lost and confused. My story had often been one of despair and loss, but it had a happy ending. Strength and resilience had won the day.

I wasn't yet in the US and a few tricky moments still awaited me. But at least, I wouldn't be on my own anymore. Sina would accompany me as far as Amsterdam and Rick, the brother-in-law I'd never met, would be my travel companion for the home stretch.

I only packed a small carry-on bag to take with me. It felt safer to travel light. A few hours before our flight, I met Sina in the hotel lobby. Holding my small suitcase, I had a huge smile on my face.

Tarik was waiting by the front desk, his eyes brimming. I gave him a quick hug goodbye, thanking him for everything he had "helped" me with. He was a pathetic creep, but I was so happy that I was ready to forgive and forget. The taxi was waiting for us outside the hotel. With a last wave of the hand, I got in and settled for the drive to the airport.

Goodbye, hotel! Goodbye, Istanbul! Now I could think ahead to the land far, far away from all my troubles where I would soon enjoy a new life with my beloved sister Roya and the rest of my family by my side. I closed my eyes and prayed for no more setbacks, no more obstacles.

CHAPTER THIRTEEN

THE TERMINAL

"Be happy for this moment. This moment is your life."
–Omar Khayyam

Standing in line at the check in counter at Istanbul's Atatürk airport, I was impatient to board my flight out of Turkey. Heavy traffic had slowed us down and we were cutting it fine, but it looked like we were going to make it.

It was a busy evening at the airport. Swarms of people were running in every direction and security lines were long. In front of us, two small kids, restless, were jumping up and down, evidently excited to get on a plane. Their exasperated parents turned and looked at us, offering a silent apology.

I smiled at them. The kids were entertaining and their enthusiasm contagious. Like them, I was thrilled to embark on my journey, but I still had niggling worries about something going wrong at the last minute. Sina's presence by my side felt reassuring.

•　　•　　•

Mainly, I was delighted to be leaving Istanbul. Don't get me wrong—Istanbul is a nice place! On my few outings with friends—and with treacherous Amin, who pretended to be on my side—I admired the city's energy, natural beauty and the depth of its history stretching back millennia. It offered me a temporary refuge, and for this I was grateful.

But the city only served as a transitional place, a waiting room that linked the old existence I was leaving behind with the new one awaiting me in California. There, surrounded by my family, pampered and supported, I would be free to pursue my artistic passions.

To give the city her dues, Istanbul provided the backdrop for significant personal growth. I was leaving it a very different woman than when I arrived, a naive and fearful 23-year-old broken into a million pieces after enduring domestic abuse for months. Not only had I found a way out, in spite of numerous hurdles, but I had also matured and grown more confident during the few months I spent here.

Here, I learned to stand on my own two feet and began a slow recovery. The few months I spent in the city on two continents were the first time in my life when I was entirely on my own. It had been rough and my mettle was often tested by loneliness and lack of progress, there was no denying it! I trusted the wrong men on several occasions and paid a heavy price. But I learned crucial lessons and started the next chapter with fire in my belly, more streetwise and determined than ever to achieve my objectives. I would not be as easily fooled again.

• • •

When Sina and I reached the front of the line, the security agent on the right asked for my passport and ticket while the person on the left checked Sina's. My documents were quickly processed and the agent waved me through. Phew! When I turned back to make sure that Sina was following me, I saw that he had been asked to step aside and was held up at the security counter. I could detect concern in his eyes. His usual confidence seemed to have slipped. What was going on? I was usually the one who got frightened and needed reassurance.

Sina was waving his hands as he talked to the man who was joined by two colleagues. From the other side of the security line, I could not make out what they were saying, but the conversation appeared heated. I was puzzled, but Sina the charmer could talk himself out of any tricky situation. No reason for me to get involved. He would catch up with me. But as I headed toward our departure gate, a security guard intercepted me. "Wait, Miss," he said. Now it was my turn to be held up!

"What is going on? What is happening?" I asked, puzzled and alarmed. I thought Sina was dealing with a bureaucratic hiccup. Could the situation be more serious? Not another obstacle, please!

Escorted by the uniformed agent, I walked back toward Sina. The color had drained from his face and he looked tense.

"What is going on," I asked point blank. Turning his head to avoid looking me in the face, he muttered, "Uh, nothing. It's just a misunderstanding."

"What do you mean?" I insisted.

He kept silent, looking strained. I glanced at the clock: Boarding time was fast approaching. I would have to make my way to the gate soon if I wanted to catch my flight. What was causing this delay?

I turned to one of the officers.

"Tell me what's going on, please!" I urged him. "My flight is leaving soon and I can't afford to miss it. What's the problem?" I asked in English, hoping he would understand. My Turkish was too limited to engage in conversation with officials.

The two agents stared at me coldly. Before answering, they exchanged a few words in Turkish. Finally, one of them offered me an explanation in broken English. Maybe he felt sorry for me. "Your friend over there is carrying drugs. We found opium in his carry-on bag."

My jaw dropped! I looked at the officer, then at Sina, in utter disbelief. You have got to be kidding! How could Sina be so stupid? He knew I was so desperate to leave Turkey and yet he would jeopardize my chances of getting out. I was livid!

The fool had not even tried to keep his trafficking away from me, so I would not be dragged into his mess. In fact, he had deliberately stood shoulder to shoulder with me in the security line, talking to me and making it known to everyone around us that we were together. Had I once again been used? Had Sina helped me get a transit visa because traveling with a woman who looked like his girlfriend would provide better cover for illegal drug trafficking?

I did not care about him or what he was doing, but I was fuming that he had put me in danger. I would NOT miss this flight! I would not end up in a Turkish jail.

Angry tears welled up in my eyes as I pleaded with the officers. This time, fury rather than despair animated me. I would not let Sina's selfishness and stupidity mess up my plans. I would find my way on that flight, no matter what.

"I swear to god, I only met this man a few days ago at my hotel," I told the officers in a shaky voice. "We just shared a cab to the airport since we were booked on the same flight. I swear to God, I hardly know him. Look, I have proof! I am flying to Panama and he lives in Holland. I promise you: I have nothing to do with him."

Initially unconvinced, the officers hesitated. I continued to make my case, all the while keeping an eye on the giant clock on the wall. It was time to board the flight. With urgent determination, I insisted. "I don't know anything about this man or what he is carrying. I'm not an accomplice. Please let me go! I can't miss my flight."

At this point, I was ready to make a run for it if they refused to let me go, but I recognized that my chances of leaving were doomed unless I could convince them that I was not party to Sina's crime.

The tone of my voice appeared to have shaken their belief that Sina and I had acted in concert. They looked at each other and ordered me to wait in the corner, away from Sina.

Rage was still boiling inside me. I turned my back so I would not have to look at Sina. My hand was itching to slap him hard and I would have done if given an opportunity. I wanted to scream at him with the full force of my lungs. "You bastard, how could you do this to me?!" Instead, I controlled my feelings, attempted to look calm and stemmed the flow from my runny nose with a tissue.

After a few minutes, one of the officials came back with my passport in hand. "You can go."

OH MY GOD! I had managed to get through to them. "Thank you very much, sir," I said. I grabbed my passport and ran as fast as my legs would allow towards my gate, without so much as a look at Sina. He would probably be taken to a police station for interrogation.

I made it. At the counter, before I entered the tunnel leading to the parked plane, the airline employee looked at my ticket and greeted me with the warmth reserved for first-class ticket holders.

•   •   •

On the plane, a flight attendant directed me to a wide leather-covered seat in the first-class section of the plane. This was only my second flight ever. The previous one had been a short hop in an older, smaller plane to Cyprus. This time, I experienced the luxury of the first-class cabin on a wide-bodied aircraft. It was a bit intimidating, but I tried to look like I belonged, remembering times in Tehran when I accompanied my wealthy friends to venues normally out of financial reach for people like me.

I looked around, curious to see who my fellow travelers were on this fancy first-class flight to Amsterdam. On the other side of the aisle, an elegantly dressed older couple greeted me with a nod. The other passengers were mostly middle-aged men in well-cut business suits, who looked like lawyers or politicians. Two other women appeared to be traveling alone, like me. I was by far the youngest passenger in the section. Although feeling slightly out of place, I did my best to conceal it.

When the engine revved up and a crew member announced our imminent departure, I sank back into my seat and allowed myself to relax. As the wheel lifted off the ground, I took a deep breath and closed my eyes. I was finally flying out of Turkey, and I was leaving in style. What a great start to the rest of my life! The butterflies in my stomach were welcome flutters of excitement, rather than the tense twists of helplessness I had often experienced.

This comfortable seat in the peaceful environment of the first-class cabin should be a first taste of what was to come—a sample of my future life. From now on, everything would be dramatically different, I swore to myself. No more lonely, sad days spent staring in space in cramped hotel rooms! I would grab everything that life had to offer with both hands. My eyes still closed, I prayed, "God, Universe, whoever is out there, let this be the last of my struggles. Please take me to my family safely. I'm tired of fighting."

My thoughts turned to Amsterdam, where I would meet my new brother-in-law for the first time the next day. I looked forward to this encounter, confident that Rick and I would immediately hit it off and bond. Without his and Roya's solid backing, I would not be on this plane. That Rick was willing to fly to The Netherlands to pick me up and accompany me on what was likely to be a tricky journey from Mexico to the US only confirmed that he was a wonderful man. He was family, as much as Roya was.

About half an hour into the flight, as I was sipping the cocktail that a courteous flight attendant had brought me as soon as we reached cruising altitude, I spotted a tall silhouette lingering by my seat. I looked up, expecting the flight attendant to offer me a refill. My heart almost stopped when I saw Sina. How had he managed to get on the flight? When I rushed to the gate, I was certain the Turkish police would hold him back and take him into custody. I should have known! This smooth operator could get himself out of almost any situation. I suspected this involved a hefty bribe in this case. In Turkey as in other countries in the region, the system was often corrupt and for the right price, you could buy anything and anyone, including the police. So, there he was, standing next to my seat with a smirk on his face. "Happy to see me?" he asked.

I was not placated by his smile. "Are you crazy? What the hell were you thinking?" I hissed.

I kept my voice down to avoid attracting attention, but my anger was spilling out. Sina's irresponsible actions nearly derailed my plans and prevented my departure. "You knew how desperately I needed to get out of Istanbul where I'd been stuck for months. Why would you put me in such a hazardous situation?" I asked.

He did not answer. He thought I would provide cover and defend him. Instead, I denied knowing him. He had a bone to pick with me. "Nice of you to say that you didn't know me," he said with a voice heavy with sarcasm. "You knew me well enough when I helped you get a transit visa to Holland."

"For god's sake! I have thanked you profusely and repeatedly for your help. That doesn't mean you had the right to make me an accomplice to your crimes! What you do is your business, but don't get innocent bystanders involved. You almost ruined everything for me. I could have been arrested and thrown in jail! Do you even understand the gravity of your actions?"

He laughed it off. "Take it easy. Nothing happened in the end."

Brushing the incident aside, he said casually, " Why don't you come and sit next to me. There's an empty seat. Looks like someone missed their flight."

How cheeky! Sina's nonchalant demeanor was irritating. He had no remorse and did not even bother to apologize for putting me in a risky position.

"No thanks," I said, annoyed. Why would I leave my comfortable first-class seat to sit in the crowded coach section for his sake? My sister had spent a lot of money for my ticket and I had no intention joining this troublemaker in economy.

"Why not? We can chat during the trip." The standoff at the security check was already in the past for him. He had moved on and could not understand that I was deeply resentful.

I collected myself and said calmly, "Because I'm comfortable here and I really don't feel like talking to you right now. You betrayed my trust."

Used to getting his own way, Sina appeared unhappy that I turned him down. I picked up the in-flight magazine and started leafing through it, eager to put an end of our conversation.

He stood by my seat for a while longer, then marched back to the economy section, disgruntled.

"You, ungrateful woman!" was his parting shot.

In his eyes, I was indebted to him. In reality, it had not cost him much to help me get a visa. For him, it was a chance to play God and demonstrate his power. I was thankful for his efforts and I owed him a debt of gratitude. Actually, I had planned to send him a thank-you gift once I reached California. But this did not mean I would forever be at his beck and call.

After enjoying a dinner and dessert served on proper china plates, with a napkin stretched across the tray like a tablecloth, I took a short nap until we drew closer to our destination.

I played around with the many buttons on the side of the seat until I eventually figured out how to turn my seat into a chaise lounge. Many of my fellow first-class passengers had already stretched out. I didn't want to expose myself as a novice traveler and had too much pride to ask the flight attendant. I wanted to maintain the illusion that I lived life in the fast lane. After all, that was my goal and here was an opportunity to practice for what was to come. This felt right: from the beginning, I enjoyed the nicer things in life and luxury gave me comfort. Even though I was pretending, I felt in my natural element.

· · ·

After landing in Amsterdam, I headed straight toward the transit area. Schiphol Airport is as big as a city, with numerous shops and restaurants. As I was looking around, trying to find my way to the hotel, I felt a hand on my shoulder. I turned around. It was Sina, again!

This time, he approached things different. "I owe you an apology," he said, apparently chastened by our previous interaction. "Let me help you get settled before I leave the airport." In spite of the humbler tone, I was hesitant to accept his help, although I recognized I could use it. The place was huge and I'd never checked into a hotel on my own.

I followed him and requested a room with two beds at the hotel front desk. My brother-in-law Rick was due to arrive the next day and he was going to spend one night here with me before we flew to Mexico together. The hotel staff was friendly and spoke fluent English. Communication would be easier during my two-night stay at Amsterdam's airport than during the months I spent in Istanbul.

There, few people spoke good English or even understood it, and my Turkish was not up to par.

Sina insisted on carrying my bag up to the room, which contained two twin beds separated by nightstand. Small and simple with a clean shower area. Perfect for a short stay!

He closed the door behind him, and sat on one of the beds, making himself comfortable. He watched as I unpacked a few things I had set aside for the overnight stay. I did not understand why he was not leaving. His persistence was triggering me. I kept busy, hoping he would pick up the signal to leave.

"Come, lie down on the bed with me for a bit," he said, breaking the silence. Here we go again. Seriously!? Did he think that I was going to sleep with him? I turned around and looked at him. At this point, I was beyond annoyed. I was amused by his oversized sense of entitlement.

"Ummm, No. Thank you. I'm going to decline your generous offer," I said with a sarcastic smile. He did not budge.

Sina kept insisting and would not give it up. I was losing my patience. I had too much on my plate and dealing with him was not something I could handle at that moment.

I snapped," Sina, the answer is no. I appreciate all your assistance and I can't thank you enough for helping me get the transit visa, but it's time for you to go."

"Why? Don't you like me? " he asked, desolate.

I took a deep breath and said, "No, I don't. Not like that. You helped me and I am forever grateful, but all I can offer is my gratitude. It's time for you to leave."

"Look, you could come to Amsterdam with me," Sina insisted. "It's not going to be easy to reach your family in California. If you stayed with me, we could get married and EU citizenship would make it a lot easier for you to get into the US. Then you could visit your family anytime you wanted. Lots of Persians live around here, you would make friends in no time."

How many proposals had I received in the past 6 months? Honestly! I was exhausted and at my wit's end. I did not feel like arguing with this idiot. What was it about these men who thought they could plan my life for me when they barely knew me?

Time to stop being nice. "That's enough," I said, curtly. "Just go before I lose my cool. Please!"

Sina stayed quiet for a few seconds, then he realized that I would not change my mind and I was not joking. Without a word, he got out and left, slamming the door behind him. Good riddance!

I locked the door, stretched out on one of the beds and let out a sigh of relief, giggling in anticipation of meeting my brother-in-law for the first time. I'd seen a million pictures of him and knew what he looked like. When I was living in the condo owned by Hamid's mom, I would stare at Roya's wedding pictures for hours, scrutinizing Rick's face and wondering, "Is he good to my sister? Is he kind?"

Now, I knew he was because he was willing to take time out to come all the way to Amsterdam to pick me up and risk criminal charges for taking me back to my family illegally. My sister, wise beyond her years, had found a good man. That he understood how close his wife and I were and was willing to go out of his way to help an unknown sister-in-law said a lot about the kind of man he was. He must love my sister a great deal to do this for her. Yes, he must be exceptional. And that brought me great comfort. I could not wait to meet him.

After a quick nap, I got dressed and left my room to explore the transit area. There was plenty to see and I could indulge in window shopping to my heart's content.

I didn't want to emulate Tom Hanks in the movie "The Terminal," stuck endlessly in an airport, but I felt I could happily spend a bit more time here. Incidentally, the movie was based on the true story of one of my compatriots, Iranian refugee Mehran Karimi Nasseri who spent eight years stranded at Paris Charles de Gaulle airport.

But thanks to my cousin's passport and the transit visa that enabled to travel as far as Amsterdam, I would not share his fate, Rick would soon take me to Mexico and then California, fingers crossed! I walked around, examined the items on the shelves of the duty-free shops and tried some lipsticks. After poking my head in several bars and restaurants, I chose one to dine in and sat at a table, enjoying the buzz of the lively crowd around me.

Freedom was beginning to feel real. I had enjoyed some liberty in Istanbul, of course, but there my situation still felt too precarious. It was too close to home, and with many Iranians traveling to Istanbul daily, I did not feel sufficiently safe. But Amsterdam was different. Now, surrounded by anonymous travelers, I could order an alcoholic drink and enjoy it without fearing the consequences. I had officially entered the Western world and was finally out of the reach of the dark forces that had stalked me.

As I waited for my meal, I took a sip of my martini—a cocktail I'd chosen at random from the menu without really knowing what it was. Looking ahead to my new life in California was exhilarating. But there was also some sadness deep down, as I knew I could probably never return to my homeland. In spite of all the difficulties I had faced there, Iran was my country and its culture was deeply embedded in my heart and soul. I had not even said goodbye to my grandmother and, as it turned out, I would never see her again. Nor would I see the friends I had grown up with. I might never walk the busy streets of Tehran again, among the millions who spoke my native tongue.

But I would have a new home! Old habits would fade, replaced by new ones. New friends who knew little about my past and my struggles would replace the familiar faces of my childhood. I would just be the new girl with an accent. I was grateful for the opportunity to live in a country where people enjoy greater rights, even if I left part of me behind.

My goal was in sight. I tricked my mind into believing that my arrival in California was a done deal, and the last leg of my long journey would be smooth. I had to keep my spirits high, and not allow myself to contemplate being busted at the US border and deported. Right now, nothing could dampen my sparkle.

CHAPTER FOURTEEN

BUMPY ROAD TO HEAVEN

"Wherever you go, east, west, north or south, think of it as a journey into yourself. The one who travels into itself travels the world."
–Shams Tabrizi

Early the next afternoon, I stood by the arrival gate, scrutinizing the faces of passengers stepping through the automatic doors.

While waiting for Rick to land in Amsterdam, I had spent a leisurely morning browsing the stores, looking at clothes, trying on sunglasses, and nervously running out when the salesperson asked if I needed any help. I was not planning on buying anything. My journey was not over yet. But I was mesmerized by the glam and glitter of it all and enjoyed window shopping. Schiphol was not Rodeo Drive or the Champs Elysées, but the abundance of luxury designer boutiques was new to me. I could have found similar stores in the upmarket districts of Istanbul, but I had not sought them out.

After a few minutes, I spotted a tall, blond, blue-eyed man who was scanning his surroundings. I recognized him right away from the wedding pictures I had studied for hours. I waved energetically and called his name to make sure I had identified the right man. "Rick?" He turned to me and broke into a huge smile when he saw me.

"Naz!!! It's so good to finally meet my sister-in-law. Come over here." He pulled me in for a long and warm embrace. It felt so good! Rick was the newest member of our family—he and my sister had only been married for a year—but I already felt I had known him forever. We had spoken often on the phone. The warm hug made me feel I had made me realized how much I had missed normal human contact and the cocoon of family. At that cathartic moment, Rick felt like home.

Rick took a step back and squinted to get a better peek at me. "Look at your blonde hair," he teased me. "We could easily pass as siblings." We both burst into laughter.

As we walked toward the hotel, we chatted happily. It felt like we had known each other for a long time, yet we had only just met. Once in our hotel room, we spent a couple of hours catching up. Rick had brought more pictures of my siblings. He also showed me the house I would live in. I wanted to hear all the latest news of my family members in California. How was Roya? Niloo and her family? Joseph? Rick was a direct link to my siblings.

. . .

Since we were not leaving until early the next morning, my brother-in-law wanted to do a quick tour of Amsterdam and catch a glimpse of its legendary canals. "Would you mind if I went out for a few hours," Rick asked. I would have loved to accompany him, but my transit visa and my Iranian passport did not allow me to leave Schiphol. I could not afford to endanger our plan and risk all the progress achieved for a night on the town. Rick, on the other hand, was welcome to enter almost any country in the world with his American passport.

Rick had never been to The Netherland and I understood his desire to take advantage of his visit, short as it was. I was only too happy to grant his request. My brother-in-law had come a long way to rescue me and I was pleased that he could at least get some personal benefit from the trip.

Before leaving, Rick handed me my cousin's passport and suggested I study it well before we left. I needed to familiarize myself with the date of birth, name, and also Sahar's signature in case I had to sign forms. I stared at my cousin Sahar picture in the passport. We weren't at all similar and I would have use the magic of makeup to make myself look like her. Her signature was quite convoluted, and I decided to practice it until I could sign official documents in her name without attracting the attention of the authorities. After an hour of practice, I felt confident that I could produce a decent copy of her scrawled signature, which was illegible.

I looked around the room and wondered where I would be the next day. I felt a mixture of excitement and anxiety, I had to be ready for whatever was in store for me. To distract me from anxious thoughts, I chose to repack my bag, even though I was traveling light and did not have much.

As I gathered my belongings, I spotted Rick's plane ticket from Amsterdam to Mexico on the nightstand between the two beds. How could he have forgotten to take this all-important document? My heart skipped a beat. Rick would need to show a valid ticket before he was allowed back into the transit area. I felt apprehensive. Something had to be done.

I suddenly had an idea: I would wait for Rick near the security desks. I grabbed his flight document, ran to the lower level and positioned myself as close as possible to the border control booths. On the other side, border guards were checking the travel documents of departing passengers. I paced back and forth between the lines, watching as one person after the other passed through the control point.

I had no clue when Rick would get back, but he would eventually have to pass through this area. I would wait, document in hand. If he ran into trouble, I could hand him his ticket and make sure he was allowed in.

A security guard eventually noticed the distressed young woman restlessly pacing the area. He approached me. "Is something the matter, Miss?" he asked. I came up with a story, which wasn't strictly true, but did not deviate too far from reality.

"My husband left to go into the city and he forgot to take his plane ticket. I'm afraid he won't be able to get back to the transit area. We are spending the night at the airport hotel before catching our flight out tomorrow morning. I don't know what to do."

The security officer took the ticket from my hand, examined it and handed it back to me. "Don't worry" He said. "I'll keep a look out for him and will let him back in! You don't need to wait for him here." In those days, pre-9/11, flashing an American passport was enough to made travel easier. These days, security is much tighter everywhere.

I let out a sigh of relief, thanked him, and went back to the room to finish packing. I knew when the guard see Rick's American passport, he would easily let him back into the airport. I wondered how different his reaction would have been if the passport had been Iranian. I shook my head, thinking of the level of Western prejudice against Iranians since the Revolution. It was unfair!

A few years later, after 9/11, I reflected again on this incident and the guard's helpful attitude toward Rick. After terrorists brought down the twin towers in

New York and attempted to attack the Pentagon, security was tightened all over the world. Post 9/11, Rick would never have gained access to the transit area without all the proper documents in hand. We were lucky that day!

I was already in bed, but unable to sleep because I was worried, when the door opened and Rick walked in, happy as a clam. He had forgotten his travel documents, but not the room key. I jumped out of bed and said, "Oh, thank god you're back!"

Rick was unfazed and he burst out laughing. "An officer greeted me at the entrance and said, 'your wife was very nervous about you not being able to get back in. She was frantically running around with your plane ticket.'" I joined in and laughed at this image of myself, running manically around the airport.

.   .   .

Now that Rick had made it back, my mind, always busy, turned to the next day and everything that could go wrong. By this time tomorrow, I could be in jail waiting to be deported back to Iran and my abusive husband's deadly grasp... or celebrating with my family in California. I was mostly concerned about Rick. What would happen to him if I got caught crossing into the United States on a passport that didn't belong to me? I did not want him arrested as an accomplice or face serious trouble for helping me. What we were doing was not a minor crime. Roya and Rick had just started their new lives together, and I would never forgive myself if things went sideways and something terrible happened to him. The stakes were very high!

After tossing and turning all night, I finally gave up trying to get some sleep and got up quietly, trying not to wake Rick up. Our flight was leaving in a couple of hours, and we didn't have far to go to reach our departure gate.

I sat in front of the mirror, pulled out my small make-up bag and opened my cousin's passport at the picture page. Using the skills, I'd developed while working on the movie in Tehran, I applied my makeup to match Sahar's picture in her passport as much as possible. We did not look alike, but passport photos are often poor reflections of the real person. My brief foray into the movie world and all those times I had spent alone in my room as a teenager experimenting with makeup and hair colors were paying off. I was about to play my biggest role, and my life depended on it.

Satisfied with my handiwork, I looked at my watch. It was time to go. I woke up Rick and packed the last few items that were laying around the room while he was taking a shower.

We checked out, stopped briefly by a café to pick up two cups of coffee and headed to our gate.

Getting on the flight to Mexico City was a breeze. Nobody cared that we were leaving Holland for Mexico. The tricky part would be entering Mexico using my cousin's passport and not getting caught. I hoped that they wouldn't pay much attention to Sahar's date of birth—she was 15 years older than me— or look too closely at the picture, comparing it with my face.

The flight itself was uneventful. Now that I was finally on my way, tiredness gained the upper hand and I fell asleep for a while. When I woke up, Rick was quietly reading next to me. He put his book down when he saw that I'd emerged from my slumber and we chatted. I had so many questions about his and Roya's life in California.

A flight attendant served us a meal—far simpler than the one I'd enjoyed in first class on the Istanbul-Amsterdam leg of the journey. We each asked for wine and raised our glasses to celebrate successfully getting on the plane together.

After the meal, Rick returned to his book while I sat pensively. I felt fidgety but didn't want to disturb Rick or raise his stress level. As our plane started its descent toward Mexico City, Rick and I went over the story we were going to tell the Mexican immigration officer at the airport, rehearsing the details a few times.

We were trying to remain outwardly relaxed and calm. Inside, we were both anxious, but we hoped we could hide our concerns from the border officials at passport control. As we left the safety of the plane, which had cut us off from the real world for half a day, Rick and I looked at each other without saying a word. We both knew exactly what was at stake and what we had to do. As a bad liar by nature, I needed to pretend to be someone else for a few minutes. The performance would be short, barely a few minutes, but it had to be Oscar-worthy, my best role ever. Whether or not I could pull it off could dramatically transform my entire life. No pressure!

.   .   .

As we stood in line, passports in hand, I could hear my heart pounding fast in my chest, as if about to jump out. It resonated so loudly within me that it seemed the entire crowd must be hearing it loud and clear. But around us, people were chatting with each other, indifferent to my heightened emotions.

Finally, we got to the front of the queue and found ourselves face to face with a Mexican officer with a stern look on his face. Not someone you would want to cross! As he opened Rick's passport, he asked, " What is your relationship with the lady?" Rick cracked a smile and answered, with his charming American accent, "She is my assistant. We went to Holland for some business. We're on our way back home to California and decided to stop in Mexico City to visit some business associates here."

The officer raised his head. "What is your business?"

"I'm in venture capital," Rick answered.

The man took a good look at Rick, raise an eyebrow and handed him his passport without saying a word.

Now it was my turn. He opened the passport at the photo page. I was feeling faint and barely able to stand up. Rick, noticing my flustered face, struck up a conversation with the officer, hoping to distract him and prevent him from paying too much attention to the passport I had submitted.

"It was very cold in Amsterdam. How is the weather here in Mexico City?" and before waiting for the officer to answer he continued, "Do you have any recommendations for us? What to see, where to eat? I have heard amazing things about your city. It is our first visit."

The officer cast a cursory look at the picture and handed me the passport. He finally cracked a smile, and gave Rick a long list of recommendations, showing no concern for the busy line of people behind us waiting behind us. After showering us with information we didn't need, the officer shook Rick's hand and said to us, "Enjoy Mexico City." We thanked him profusely and walked away, exchanging a complicit hand squeeze to express our relief.

We had no intention of staying in Mexico City. Rick and I were moving to another section of the airport and catching a domestic flight to Tijuana.

We didn't have to wait long before it was time to board the next plane. I was rapidly becoming a jet setter! When we were in the air and the flight attendants took our orders, Rick ordered two tequila drinks to celebrate our huge victory. We had cleared one major hurdle. "You've had tequila before, right?" he asked.

"Hmmm, No. I can't say I have. We mostly drink vodka in Iran. And in Turkey, they mostly drink raki". "What is Raki?" He asked making a funny face. "It's nasty and tastes of aniseed," I said scrunching my nose up. " But it's Turkey's national drink and after a while, you get used to the taste." Rick was listening to my explanation curiously so I continued, "But it's not worse than the vodka we drank back home, which was often made by some random person in their basement because alcohol is illegal in Iran, you know?" Rick shook his head and said, "Yes of course, Roya has told me about all that."

The flight attendant arrived with two tiny tequila bottles and two cups filled with ice. Rick poured the drinks, looked at me with a smile, and said, "I am about to change your life, young lady," he said. "You're going to love this." Before I could take a sip, he asked, "Wait, how do you say cheers in Persian?" I smiled and answered, "Salamati." We clicked our glasses and I gulped down my first— but not last—tequila.

For the remainder of the flight, we drank some more, told each other stories, laughed, joked, and talked about the life I left behind, and the life I was about to start. The alcohol was relieving our tension, but we were not yet off the hook. There was still one more border to cross, overland this time: the Tijuana-San Diego border. Every day, countless refugees from Mexico attempt the crossing illegally, in search of a more secure life. They were not so different from me. And because of the amount of illegal activity at this border, officials were constantly on alert. Crossing into the US would not be easy.

·   ·   ·

When we landed in Tijuana, Rick and I were both a little buzzed on tequila, as well as high on the adrenaline of this journey. Neither of us were used to acting outside the law, even if I had sneaked out of Iran without my husband's permission.

As we stepped out of Tijuana airport, I saw a familiar face nervously searching the crowd. I knew those eyes. I knew that face. It was the face I had looked up to all my life. Those were the eyes I looked into when I first regained consciousness after trying to take my own life. Roya, my beloved sister, was waiting for us!

Rick had not told me that Roya would come to greet us in Tijuana. What an amazing surprise! My big sister would be with us for the perilous drive across the US border.

I dropped my suitcase on the ground and ran towards her. We hugged and we cried as Rick looked on, giving us the space and the time we needed to savor our reunion. Neither of us could say a word. I looked at my beautiful sister. The last time I had seen her was at Tehran airport. I had just got engaged to Hamid and she was leaving Iran. So much had happened in the intervening years.

The tremendous efforts Roya had deployed over the past few months to get me to safety were not lost on me. I was lonely and miserable while my life was in limbo in Istanbul, but Roya had suffered too and worried about me day and night. Now we were together!

As we clumsily walked towards the car, our arms still wrapped tight around each other, we knew we were not yet in the clear. The risk that we could be torn apart again was real and we were both fearful. But I was relieved she would be by my side when I faced the last test.

Roya got in the driver seat; Rick sat on the front passenger seat while I crawled in the back of their dark green jeep Cherokee. In the car, Rick and I briefly filled in Roya on our trip from Amsterdam, but it was not long until we reached the US border post. As we slowed down to take our place in the queue, Roya looked at me in the rear-view mirror and said, " Naz, no matter what, stay calm and let Rick do all the talking." I nodded to let her know I understood. "All you have to say is "YES" to the border security when they ask if you are an American citizen," she continued. "Do you understand me?" Her tone was urgent and I nodded again. My entire body felt tense. I'd overcome many obstacles, but this last hurdle felt like the most challenging. It would be too cruel if fate denied me my freedom at the last moment.

There was a massive line of cars at the border trying to cross into California. Border security guards were carefully examining travel documents and inspecting each car, walking around every vehicle with fierce dogs that looked like wolves. This was a major hub for drug and people smuggling into the US and security was tight.

One of the border security officers approached our car. Roya rolled down her window and I looked away. I was afraid to make eye contact, scared that the officer would read the fear on my face and get suspicious.

While he took a look inside the car, Rick started a conversation in a friendly tone of voice. "Officer, how are you doing tonight?" The white officer seemed pleased. Among the many Mexicans trying to cross the border, Rick stood out with his straight blond hair, blue eyes, and good ol' American accent. border guard probably viewed him as a breath of fresh air. The officer then poked his head inside the car to look at the back seat and saw another blonde. "I'm fine, thank you for asking!" The officer replied. Then he turned to Rick and asked, "All American Citizens?" All three of us answered in harmony, "Yes!"

"WELCOME HOME," he said as he got out of our way to let us pass.

We drove away, rolled up the windows, and as soon as we were far enough and out of earshot, we screamed with happiness and excitement.

"So, this is it? It's over?" I asked, grinning from ear to ear. Rick and Roya looked at each other. After a brief pause, Roya said, "Well, almost."

"Almost? Is there another border?" I asked, my smile fading away.

"It's not a border" Rick explained. " It's just a checkpoint. But most of the time it's not even open, so don't worry. With luck, the checkpoint won't be manned."

By then, it was dark outside and I could not see much. I wanted to drink in the scenery and catch my first glimpse of America. If guards were going to stop me and send me back after discovering my false identity at this last checkpoint, I wanted to at least see a bit of the land I tried so hard to reach—a land that had welcomed my whole family and become a new home for them but seemed not to want me. This land, a nation of immigrants from all over the world, welcomed misfits and took in misunderstood souls, and made many dreams come true. Would I be allowed to experience The American Dream?

We were getting closer. I could see bright lights in the distance, and cars were slowing down. The checkpoint, often unmanned, must be open! As we slowed down, two guards walked along the line of vehicles—one on the right side of the cars, and one on the left. Carrying a handgun at their waist, they each had a flashlight that they pointed inside the cars as they slowly rolled through. As our turn came, the officer on the right took a cursory look inside our vehicle before waving his hand in the air to keep driving. No need to stop. Roya pushed on the gas pedal and accelerated. We took off like runaway bandits!

When the lights behind us disappeared in the distance, Roya turned around, looked at me, and said, "That was it, sis! No more borders, no more checkpoints. We did it. You can finally relax." Rick twisted his body to look at me, held my hand, and said "Welcome to the United States of America!"

Overjoyed but suddenly feeling subdued after months of effort, I sat back on my seat, stared out of the window. Gradually, the tension I had felt for months receded and my heart stopped pounding. I whispered to myself, "Welcome to the United States of America" and I smiled at my reflection in the window.

• • •

An hour later, we turned into what seemed a dark back alley and stopped in an old garage.

I got out of the car and followed Roya through a little door that connected the garage to the house. It was a charming little bungalow: two bedrooms, a small kitchen, and a cozy living room, modestly decorated. Rick took my suitcase to one of the rooms and said, "This is your room. I hope you like it." My smile said it all. "Are you serious?! I have been living in a tiny hotel room for the past few months. You could put me in the basement and I'd still be happy." Roya and Rick burst out laughing.

My new room had a full-size bed and a nightstand with a vintage lamp. Its walls were decorated with small paintings of the ocean and seashells and a colorful rug covered the floor. I could tell Roya and Rick had tried to make this room as comfortable and welcoming as possible. Such a stark contrast with the hostile environments where I had spent most of the past few months. Closed curtains hid a door at the other side of the room—did it lead to a terrace or balcony? It was dark outside and I was bone tired. I would find that out in the morning. As I sat on my new bed, I saw that it was almost 2:00 AM. I was ready to sleep. It had been a very, very long day.

"Get some sleep, we have a lot of catching up to do tomorrow. Niloo and Joseph are also going to drop by to see you." Roya said before going into her bedroom.

I undressed and climbed into bed. It was a chilly night and I pulled up the blanket all the way to my chin and immediately fell into a deep sleep.

The next morning, I woke up to an unfamiliar sound and felt a little disoriented when I opened my eyes. For an instant, I could not remember where I was. Then, as I looked around, I remembered: I am in California. I am at Rick and Roya's home in Newport. I'm with my family. I am safe and free!

My heart leapt with joy at this thought and a feeling of deep contentment spread through my body. After months of efforts, after all that I and my family had been through, I had made it. Our hard work didn't go to waste. We pulled it off and I had a chance to turn a page on my life and start a brand-new chapter, in a new country, among people who loved me.

I jumped out of the bed and opened the curtains. The brightness outside made me blink. I rubbed my eyes and tried to identify the sound that had woken me up.

I slid the glass door and stepped outside. My feet sank into a soft, grainy surface. I looked down and saw that I was standing on a bed of sand. Straight in front of me was the Pacific Ocean and the sound I had heard was that of small waves softly crashing on the beach after forming little peaks of foam. I was mesmerized, in awe. This magnificent body of water, shining deep blue under the sun, was right outside my bedroom patio. The view was breathtaking.

I walked towards the water, feeling each grain of sand between my toes, mesmerized by the beauty in front of me. It was almost December and it was a nice day for the season. Where I came from, December days brought cold weather and snow. But here in Southern California, everything was different.

I reached the edge of the water, sat down, and gazed into the distance, my heart bursting with gratitude. As my eyes welled up with tears of joy, I thought back on all the hardship I'd experienced to get here, the mistakes I had made, the pain I had experienced. I had fought hard battles and felt crushing loneliness over the past few years. I would never feel alone again and nothing could cause me such pain anymore.

As I reflected on the traumatic events of the past few years, I realized that surrounded by people who loved me, I would always be safe. I was oceans away from the monster Hamid had turned into, and a world away from the tyrants who ruled my country. As waves receded into the wide ocean after reaching the beach, they took away my dark memories.

Building a new life here would not be easy. I had to brace myself for new battles, legal this time. It would not be easy to obtain asylum and avoid deportation. But as long as I had my family by my side, I could face whatever was thrown my way. I was going to be completely honest with the immigration office, tell them my whole story and how I got to the US. I could rest a little easier knowing that respect for human rights meant something here. I would not be discriminated against just on the basis of my gender and I knew I would get a fair hearing.

I got up and ran back towards the house and the life that was awaiting me. I turned my back on the past. I would not be defined by it. I was open to a future that was as yet undetermined but offered great promise. I could follow my passions, learn new skills and choose a career that fulfilled me. I had escaped from hell and would earn my spot in heaven, in the land of the free—if the land of the free would have me.

EPILOGUE

"Sorrow prepares you for joy. It violently sweeps everything out of your
house, so that new joy can find space to enter."
–Rumi

When I first settled in California, still bruised by my abusive marriage
and my country's refusal to recognize my rights as a woman, I closed
the Iran chapter of my life and threw myself into becoming an
American in all aspects. At the time, I did not feel like I belonged. America was
nothing like how I expected it to be. It was just so...big. I had little in common
with the Iranian Americans in California, most of them children of the privileged
classes who had fled decades earlier.

My first priority was to swap the British-accented English I had been taught
at school in Tehran for the local slang. I also needed to regularize my status. Soon
after my arrival, I applied for the right to live in the US legally and later obtained a
green card. Then I had to become financially independent, even if continued to
live in Rick and Roya's welcoming home for a while.

One of my first jobs in the US was at the beauty counter of Macy's. I learned
a lot from my colleagues, developed a network and nurtured new friendships—
some of them still strong more than two decades later. Interacting with Americans
helped me to integrate. It was easier to re-invent myself in their company than
among fellow Iranians.

To my American buddies, I was an exotic friend from a far-away land. They
knew little about my country of origin and asked few questions about my past,
but they took me under their wing and delighted in filling the gaps in my
knowledge of American culture. We were all in our early twenties and, like a late
bloomer, I learned a lot from them.

I walked my own path, attending college for the first time at the age of 28, I decided to attend a school for Fashion and Design. I did not have a lot in common with the 18-year-old boys and girls I attended class with, but I loved fashion school and was determined to make the most of this opportunity. I had found my passion, and quickly after graduating turned it into a lucrative styling business.

With each small triumph, I grew more confident and bolder, rediscovering that rebellious little girl who played soccer with the boys in Tehran and drew horns on a portrait of Ayatollah Khomeini. In my new homeland, my strong will and ambition were considered assets, not character flaws to be tamed.

The day I finally obtained US citizenship, in my early thirties, was glorious. With my new blue passport and its eagle seal, I could fly around the world and enjoy the rights and protections enshrined in the US Constitution. I had arrived at my destination. I was free at last!

. . .

After my arrival in the US, I lived and worked near my parents and siblings around Newport Beach, California. Life was comfortable in this wealthy beach community, which was home to some rich and famous figures like the late basketball player Kobe Bryant, one of America's most successful and loved athletes.

Being surrounded by caring relatives helped me heal. Little by little, I started acquiring clients for my budding styling business, mostly wealthy women living in Newport's beautiful waterside mansions, and a couple from the Real Housewives of Orange County. I was becoming successful in the area. I enjoyed mingling with the handsome tanned surfers and blonde girls who frequented beach restaurants and art galleries.

After the end of a six-year relationship, followed by the loss of my dad, I needed a change, however. Dad's passing was a huge hit. We often clashed in my youth, but I was still his baby daughter and I had never lost anyone that close to me before. I was able to care for him in his final months and had made peace with my mother.

When my mom visits me in Los Angeles, we enjoy watching old Iranian movies together. They trigger conversations about the old days, the actors we used to admire and bring back memories of my dad. Leaving Iran behind was far harder for my parents than it was for me and my siblings. As time passes, I realize that joining us in the US was an extraordinary act of self-sacrifice on the part of my parents. Being close to their children and grandchildren and offering them support came naturally to them, so they never questioned it or drew attention to its emotional cost. Leaving their familiar environment must have been heart wrenching. My dad hated Iran's Islamic regime and railed against it, but he loved his country in spite of the difficult living conditions. Until his death, he remains an Iranian man through and through—old-fashioned, often demanding and cantankerous, but ultimately loving in his own way, and determined to look out for his family.

Time had come to spread my wings and try something new. I had outgrown Newport Beach, and everything about Los Angeles lived up to my girlhood expectations and my passion for TV and film. I was tired of dressing rich housewives and loved the Hollywood scene.

From the moment I arrived in California, the pull of the big city, the world capital of the entertainment industry, was strong. I attended fashion school in Los Angeles. I used to drive to the city at least twice a week to go shopping or spend time in clubs and trendy LA restaurants with my friends. I commuted for an hour and a half each way to work with a famous actress and model. I loved Los Angeles and now was the moment to put down roots in the City of Angels and achieve my lifelong ambition.

Moving away from my family was challenging after being forcibly separated from them in the past. Cutting that cord felt daunting.

"Naz, you're only going to be an hour away!" said my exasperated sisters, who had heard me express the hope of living and working in Hollywood countless times. "If you hate it you can always come back."

I found a cute little apartment and once settled started networking in the neighborhood. Arriving in Los Angeles a complete unknown was not easy, but I was intentional about putting myself out there and started getting noticed by people of influence, from style icons and journalists to A-list actors. *People Magazine* profiled me in a small article. Behind the scenes I was already helping an actress with her fashion line. What I wanted most was to expand my business and work primarily with figures of the movie world, collaborative clients whose lives and careers I could benefit directly. As it was, it felt like I was operating on the perimeter, and I had come to Los Angeles for something more.

In local coffee shops, at the gym and cocktail parties, I met people working in the film industry and gradually became friends with a few influential figures in the community. Making friends who were already stablished in the business opened doors and presented opportunities to work with a few celebrities and start my work as a celebrity stylist. Stylistically, creatively and spiritually, I had reached my true home.

I still felt something was missing in spite of my achievements. I yearned to do more. Witnessing other women telling their painful stories had helped me cope with my traumatic past. I realized that recounting my own journey could help others who felt isolated and alone.

.   .   .

Having found my place and achieved my goal gave me the strength to revisit the past. For close to two decades, I had neglected my Persian heritage while I focused on adopting American culture and integrating in my new environment. Also, in my mind, the trauma of living under a repressive regime and suffering marital abuse had come to epitomize my home country in its entirety. I could not distinguish the good from the bad and never shared memories of my past with my American friends.

But in recent years, I have felt secure enough to look back and re-examine my old life. In the ledger of events, the painful episodes recounted in this book still dominate, but time has blunted the pain. Now that I have found my place and feel comfortable with myself and my position in life, I can acknowledge my culture and traditions and how they have contributed to shaping me.

The urge to reconnect with my homeland crept in slowly. I began opening up to my close friends in California, releasing snippets of information about my childhood and early life when they asked. They saw me in a different light and kept asking more questions. I never thought my story was special: So many women around the world face worse injustice and violence. But my friends saw it differently.

"You should be so proud," they told me. "Can't you see what you've achieved?"

They urged me to write this book. I never felt I was a warrior or even brave. During tough times, I just tried to survive, one day at a time. But with the support of those close to me, I came to see that my own experiences could encourage other women in difficult situations and give them hope.

Facing up to the past, good and bad, has enabled me to reclaim the Iranian facets of my identity, sealed off in the recesses of my brain. My renewed interest in my country of origin led me to seek out old friends from back home, now living in Paris, Toronto, Munich, London or Istanbul. Reconnecting with them after decades has brought me unexpected joy. We had created warm memories together, even as we raged against the constraints imposed upon us. The authorities tried hard, but they could not kill the natural optimism of youth.

"Naz, do you remember the day we were on our way to Mona's house and the Morality Police nearly caught us carrying VHS tapes of the latest pop music clips?"

Today, we can laugh together as we reminisce about these near misses— regular occurrences during our teenage years. Our appetite for life led us astray and put us at risk, but we were united by solid bonds of friendships that still endure. Somehow, the limitations we rebelled against have strengthened these ties.

Remembering these aspects of my life in Iran has been important for my personal growth. I was always aware that I was different from my US-born friends, even if we shared American citizenship. We did not watch the same TV series while growing up, and I never enjoyed the thrill of prom night because high school graduation is not celebrated that way in Iran. I was between worlds and needed to express a side of my personality that I had kept hidden.

Positive memories are now flooding back and I cherish them. I had forgotten how much I missed my childhood friends. We speak a common language that goes beyond Farsi, our mother tongue. It extends to an entire culture. Our deep and longstanding ties warm my heart today and make me feel whole.

Unlike most of my school friends, who regularly return to Iran where they still have relatives, I have never gone back. My family is here in California and I feel fortunate to have them around me. My dad is buried here, next to his brother. This book is about my personal path, but it also reflects the trials of millions of Iranians—and of migrants all over the world—forced to leave their country. It is also a story of families, friends and lovers torn apart by political forces they have no control over.

Along with rekindling old friendships, I am rediscovering Iranian culture, music and movies, embracing my roots a bit more every day. They are part of who I am today—an American citizen with Persian blood coursing through her veins, proud of her birthplace, culture and background.

.　　.　　.

When I arrived in the US, I was still married to Hamid according to Iranian law. It hardly mattered because he no longer had power over me.

Before leaving Tehran, I had given my father power of attorney to handle my divorce. My parents told me after I had been living in California that Hamid's controlling mother had contacted them, begging for my return. Her precious son had unraveled after my departure, his behavior spiraling further out of control. They wanted me back. Parvin even promised to treat me better.

Stuck in Istanbul at the time, I was not yet out of danger and my parents kept my whereabouts secret. They pretended I was still living with them in Iran.

Once I took up residence in the US and sorted out my legal status, I gathered enough courage to call Hamid and his mother. I needed them to know that I had escaped from their grip. Hearing their voices on the phone gave me chills. In the course of the conversation, they played it nice at first and tried to cajole me into going back to Hamid. Then, they grew angry and upset before settling on disbelief: I was lying. I could not have left!

In the face of their denials, my message was clear.

"I will NEVER return," I told them.

Whether or not Hamid was ready to grant me a divorce made little difference to me. It took him years to accept that I was well and truly gone!

Eventually, he must have decided that severing legal ties would benefit him. Maybe he had plans to re-marry. Whatever his reasons for changing his mind, by the time my ex finally took steps to end our marriage, my parents had also left Iran. The power of attorney I had given to my father had passed on to my uncle, his youngest brother, uncle Ali. He was the one who signed the divorce papers, signaling my official release from a marriage I had long consigned to personal history.

.　　.　　.

I am now living the life I dreamed about as a young girl trying to survive war and repression in the streets of Tehran.

I need to tell my story for those little girls sitting at home who think this fantasy world is out of their reach. I want them to know that behind the enjoyable glitz, we all have a complicated journey. The path is not always clear and easy, but if you hold on to your dreams, no matter how big, and fight to achieve them, you too can reach for the stars.

I found the courage to branch out on my own in West Hollywood, where I managed to make the connections to launch my own business serving influential figures of the movie world. Being a stylist is not always as glamorous as most people assume. The environment is fiercely competitive, and I do a lot of running around between stores and fashion houses. I am constantly battling LA traffic as I put together looks and bring them to my clients. Spending long hours on a film set can be exhausting. But I love it!

My happiness comes from working hard and being free to speak my truth. Is my life perfect? Of course not. There is always room for improvement. But I have close friends, family and, above all a relationship with myself that is healthy and sane. I can find joy in the simplest of liberties, like taking to Twitter to freely speak my mind about subjects I am passionate about, just because I can!

Occasionally, I get reminders of what I have escaped. Iran is often in the news for the wrong reasons and women still face serious discrimination. When I read that the outstanding female coach of the Iranian female ski team was prevented from traveling abroad to support the athletes she had trained in competition, because her husband denied her permission to leave the country, I got flashbacks. After all these years, this is still going on!

It makes me even more grateful to have been able to shape my own life. Now I want to give back and help others who deserve to enjoy the same pleasures and basic rights. I use my own struggles to shine a light on domestic violence, gaslighting, stalking and the sexual harassment of women at home, in the workplace and the public sphere. I can support the MeToo movement and add my voice to those speaking out against abuses of women and children, particularly through the use of religion. It is now my mission to educate young girls and women of all ages about domestic abuse and tell them that coercive control is not love. I hope that my story will inspire some of them and show that it is possible to walk out of a situation that appears hopeless.

Today I embrace my entire history and the personal trajectory that brought me from Tehran to Los Angeles—all that I was, am and will become. My unique circumstances, my ordeals and my long journey have made me the person I am today.

ACKNOWLEDGMENTS

I am forever grateful to my mother, my sisters, my brother, and Richard for their continued love and support, and to my dad watching from above.

Thank you to my amazing, loyal friends who encouraged me to write my story. They have supported me in this journey, and stood by my side, and have given me the strength to keep going.

Special Thanks to Nicole Pope, an amazing editor and collaborator.

And to Asal Shahindoust for her talent and knowledge.

Thank you for believing in me.

ABOUT THE AUTHOR

Naz Meknat is a Los Angeles based celebrity stylist. Her life and career could not be further removed from her perilous past in Iran. She's been operating in the fashion industry for over 15 years. It is a career of glamour Naz never dared to dream about when she was growing up in post-Revolutionary Tehran. Naz actively volunteers in her community serving as a member of many nonprofit organizations.

NOTE FROM THE AUTHOR

Word-of-mouth is crucial for any author to succeed. If you enjoyed *7000 Miles to Freedom*, please leave a review online—anywhere you are able. Even if it's just a sentence or two. It would make all the difference and would be very much appreciated.

Thanks!
Naz Meknat

Thank you so much for checking out
one of our **Memoirs**.
If you enjoy this book, please check out our recommended title for your
next great read!

Tell Me Why You Fled
by Karen O'Reilly

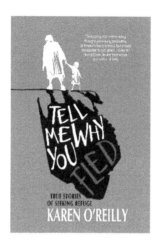

Semifinalist for the Kore Press Memoir Award

View other **Black Rose Writing** titles at
www.blackrosewriting.com/books and use promo code
PRINT to receive a **20% discount** when purchasing.

Made in the USA
Las Vegas, NV
26 August 2021